"Root champions Douglass as an important legal and political thinker, a determined fighter for full citizenship rights and freedom for all Americans regardless of race."
—J. D. SMITH, *Choice*

"Refreshing and thoughtful, written in accessible prose. It would be an excellent starting point for any undergraduate class not only on Douglass but also the debates over slavery into which he entered."
—J. W. MILLS, *Intellectual History Review*

"Is the Constitution an antislavery 'glorious liberty document' or a proslavery 'agreement with hell'? The antebellum debates between William Lloyd Garrison and Frederick Douglass are as relevant today as they were two centuries ago. In this important new book, Damon Root methodologically and accessibly walks you through this formative constitutional debate and shows why Douglass rightfully belongs 'in the pantheon of American civic philosophers.'"
—JOSH BLACKMAN, professor of constitutional law at South Texas College of Law Houston

"Damon Root has written a meticulously researched celebration of the intellectual legacy of Frederick Douglass. . . . As we continue to debate the legacy of slavery, Root convincingly argues that in reconciling the country's most profound moral incongruity—that a nation purporting to be a beacon of liberty could be so inextricably rooted in human bondage—Douglass should be mentioned in the same breath as the Founding Fathers, perhaps even more so, as a historical figure who not only championed the ideas that made America great, but in pointing out where it fell short of those values demanded that the country become a better version of itself."
—RADLEY BALKO, investigative journalist at the *Washington Post* and coauthor of *The Cadaver King and the Country Dentist: A True Story of Injustice*

T0015422

A GLORIOUS LIBERTY

A GLORIOUS LIBERTY

Frederick Douglass and the Fight
for an Antislavery Constitution

DAMON ROOT

Potomac Books

AN IMPRINT OF THE UNIVERSITY OF NEBRASKA PRESS

© 2020 by Damon Root

All rights reserved. Potomac Books is an imprint of the
University of Nebraska Press.

First Nebraska paperback printing: 2023

Library of Congress Cataloging-in-Publication Data
Names: Root, Damon, author.
Title: A glorious liberty: Frederick Douglass and the fight for
an antislavery constitution / Damon Root.
Other titles: Frederick Douglass and the fight for an
antislavery constitution
Description: Lincoln: Potomac Books, an imprint of the
University of Nebraska Press, [2020] |
Includes bibliographical references and index.
Identifiers: LCCN 2019058143
ISBN 9781640122352 (hardback)
ISBN 9781640125735 (paperback)
ISBN 9781640123816 (epub)
ISBN 9781640123823 (mobi)
ISBN 9781640123830 (pdf)
Subjects: LCSH: Douglass, Frederick, 1818–1895. | United
States. Constitution. 13th Amendment. | United States.
Constitution. 14th Amendment. | United States. Constitution.
15th Amendment. | Antislavery movements—United States—
History—19th century. | African American abolitionists. |
Abolitionists—United States. | Constitutional history—
United States.
Classification: LCC E449.D75 R66 2020 | DDC 973.8092—dc23
LC record available at https://lccn.loc.gov/2019058143

Set in Arno Pro by Laura Buis.

For Allison and Zoe

Contents

A GLORIOUS LIBERTY

Introduction

Frederick Douglass's Constitution

O n May 9, 1851, the leading lights of the abolitionist movement gathered in Syracuse, New York, for the eighteenth
annual meeting of the American Anti-Slavery Society.
Among the items on the agenda was a resolution calling for the society to officially recommend several antislavery publications, including a small weekly called the *Liberty Party Paper*. But William Lloyd
Garrison, the powerful editor of the *Liberator*, one of abolitionism's
flagship publications, would have none of that. The *Liberty Party
Paper*, Garrison complained, saw the Constitution as an antislavery
document. That view was tantamount to heresy, as it clashed with
Garrison's famous judgment that the Constitution was a proslavery
"covenant with death and an agreement with hell."[1] So a more con-
genial resolution was soon proposed: the American Anti-Slavery
Society would only recommend those publications that toed the
Garrisonian line.

It was at this point that Frederick Douglass stood up. An escaped
former slave, an internationally acclaimed orator, and the author of a
widely celebrated autobiography, Douglass cut a commanding figure
in the abolitionist ranks. And for the previous ten years, he had been
a friend, an ally, even a self-declared disciple of Garrison's. "Every
week the *Liberator* came, and every week I made myself master of
its contents," Douglass later recalled. "I not only liked—I *loved* this
paper, and its editor."[2] But Douglass no longer loved what Garrison

had to say about the Constitution. In fact, he now thought Garrison was dead wrong on the subject. What is more, Douglass decided that the time had come for him to say so in public. Douglass "felt honor bound to announce at once," he explained to the assembled worthies, that the paper he edited, the *North Star*, "no longer possessed the requisite qualification for their official approval and commendation." The Constitution, he told them, "should be wielded in behalf of emancipation."[3]

Those words went down about as well as might have been expected given the audience. There were howls of outrage, cries of censure. Garrison, for his part, accused Douglass of harboring ulterior (read, financial) motives. "There is roguery somewhere!"[4] Garrison exclaimed. Douglass never quite forgave his old comrade for that.

In truth, Douglass agonized over his change of opinion. His came around gradually and only after much brooding. He forced himself "to re-think the whole subject," he recalled, "and to study, with some care, not only the just and proper rules of legal interpretation, but the origin, design, nature, rights, powers, and duties of civil government, and also the relations which human beings sustain to it."[5]

Those studies began to produce fruit as early as 1849. Writing in the *North Star* on March 16 of that year, Douglass conceded that the Constitution "is not a proslavery instrument" when interpreted "standing alone, and construed *only* in the light of its letter." The trouble came when he considered the proslavery "opinions of the men who framed and adopted it."[6] How to reconcile the text of the Constitution with the unwritten intentions of its framers?

A year later, on April 5, 1850, Douglass moved a little further away from the strict Garrisonian position. The Constitution is "at war with itself," he now wrote. "Liberty and Slavery—opposite as Heaven and Hell—are both in the Constitution." *Both* in the Constitution? The imperious Garrison would not like the sound of that. Furthermore, Douglass ventured, "if we adopt the preamble [to the Constitution], with Liberty and Justice, we must repudiate the enacting clauses, with Kidnapping and Slavery."[7]

By 1851 his mind was made up. Yes, the Constitution did contain certain oblique references to slavery, such as the notorious Three-

Fifths Clause, which said that for purposes of taxation and political representation, state populations would be "determined by adding to the whole Number of free Persons, including those bound to Service for a Term of Years, and excluding Indians not taxed, three fifths of all other Persons." But that clause, and the handful of others like it, spoke only in the ambiguous language of *persons*. Neither the word *slave* nor the word *slavery* appeared anywhere in the text of the Constitution. That textual absence, Douglass concluded, was a fatal weakness in the slaveholders' position that must be exploited. "Take the Constitution according to its plain reading," he insisted. "I defy the presentation of a single pro-slavery clause in it. On the other hand, it will be found to contain principles and purposes, entirely hostile to the existence of slavery."[8] In the years to come, Douglass would deploy those principles and purposes against the peculiar institution until it was finally destroyed.

Arguing about slavery was a combat sport in those days, both figuratively and literally, and the field was crowded with skilled combatants. Their ranks included not only fiery abolitionists like William Lloyd Garrison but also shrewd political operators such as John C. Calhoun, the legendary South Carolina statesman who proclaimed slavery to be a positive good, one that deserved to be fully sanctioned by the Constitution and fully shielded by the powers of the federal government.

Douglass would face them both down. "Garrison sees in the Constitution precisely what John C. Calhoun sees there," Douglass observed.[9] *He* saw something different. "Interpreted as it ought to be interpreted," Douglass declared, "the Constitution is a glorious liberty document."[10]

Today Frederick Douglass is perhaps best remembered for his courageous and inspiring life story. That is merited, of course. His remarkable odyssey from slavery to freedom shines a searing and unforgettable light on some of the worst and best aspects of American history. But Douglass deserves to be remembered for much more than that. He deserves to be remembered as a significant legal and political thinker in his own right, as an intellectual firebrand who spent the better part of his life grappling with fundamental questions about the meaning of freedom and the role of government—questions that still remain powerfully relevant today.

For that reason, this book places Douglass's constitutional thought at the forefront of his extraordinary life and career, exploring how Douglass's fight for an antislavery Constitution helped to shape the course of U.S. law and politics in the nineteenth century and beyond. In the pages that follow, I hope to show that Douglass deserves to be ranked alongside Thomas Jefferson, James Madison, Alexander Hamilton, and Abraham Lincoln in the pantheon of American civic philosophers.

At a time when the principles of the Constitution and the Declaration of Independence were under assault, Douglass picked up their banner, championing inalienable rights for all, regardless of race. At a time when Americans were killing each other on the battlefield, Douglass lobbied the Lincoln administration to fight for a cause greater than the mere preservation of the Union. "No war but an Abolition war," he maintained. "No peace but an Abolition peace."[11] In the aftermath of the Civil War, when state and local governments were violating the rights of the recently emancipated, Douglass preached the importance of "the ballot-box, the jury-box, and the cartridge-box," in the fight against Jim Crow.[12]

Frederick Douglass, the former slave who secretly taught himself how to read, would teach the American people a thing or two about the true meaning of the Constitution. This book will tell the story of how he did it.

1

"A Faithful Disciple of William Lloyd Garrison"

It was a Monday, February 6, 1837, and Congressman John Quincy Adams of Massachusetts was preparing to make a heap of trouble inside the House of Representatives. Adams was not exactly your typical troublemaker. At sixty-nine, he was one of the oldest lawmakers around; he was also one of the most distinguished. His father, John Adams, hardly needed an introduction: revolutionary leader, founding father, second president of the United States. His mother, Abigail Adams, was a revered political figure in her own right. Their son, to nobody's surprise, had entered the family business and risen to the top, serving as a foreign minister under President James Madison, as secretary of state under President James Monroe, and finally as president himself, the sixth man to hold the office, elected in 1824 after losing the popular vote to Andrew Jackson but then winning the White House after the contest was decided by the House of Representatives.

Ex-presidents tend to retire quietly, if reluctantly, from the political stage. John Quincy Adams stuck around for a second act. By February 1837 he was fully immersed in his new role as a duly elected member of the lower house of Congress. And now the congressman from Massachusetts had a certain matter he wished to bring to the attention of his colleagues. Adams began by introducing a "petition of nine ladies of Fredericksburg, in the State of Virginia." He "would not name" the ladies, he said, "because, from the disposition which at present prevailed in the country," he "did not know what might happen to them if" he did reveal their names. "It was a petition," Adams said, "praying Congress to put a stop to the slave trade in the District of Columbia."[1]

Then, while his fellow representatives were still chewing on that, Adams dropped his bombshell. The *Congressional Globe* reports that he also "held in his hand a paper on which, before it was presented," he "desired to have the decision of the Speaker. It was a petition," Adams declared, "from twenty-two persons, declaring themselves to be slaves."[2]

That got everybody's attention. Indeed, all hell promptly broke loose in the chamber. "The Representatives of the slaveholding States," thundered Alabama congressman Dixon Lewis, "should *demand* that the *attempt to introduce such a petition* should instantly put in requisition the power of the House to punish the member for such an attempt." Lewis, in other words, wanted the House to slap a formal censure on the former president. And that was not all. "If this is not done," Lewis added, "and that promptly, every member from the slave States should immediately, *in a body, quit this House,* and go home to their constituencies. We have no longer any business here."[3] There would be more threats of disunion in the days to come.

This was not the first time that the House of Representatives had been rocked by a petition pertaining to slavery. On December 18, 1835, Congressman William Jackson of Massachusetts had presented "a petition from sundry citizens of Massachusetts, praying Congress to provide for the immediate abolition of slavery within the District of Columbia."[4] Rising in response, James Henry Hammond of South Carolina moved "that the petition be not received."[5] Hammond's motion was unprecedented. As a normal matter of business, the House formally received hundreds, sometimes even thousands, of petitions each year from the American people, each one requesting some sort of action on a particular issue. For a petition to "be not received" would fly in the face of this long-standing congressional practice. It would also fly in the face of the First Amendment to the U.S. Constitution, which, among other things, guaranteed "the right of the people . . . to petition the Government for a redress of grievances."

Hammond saw things differently. He could "not sit there," he said, "and see the rights of the Southern people assaulted day after day, by the ignorant fanatics from whom these memorials proceed."[6] Waddy Thompson Jr. of South Carolina was equally apoplectic. "I will not condescend to vindicate to this House or elsewhere, this or any other of our domestic institutions," he announced, employing a common euphemism for slavery. "It is no affair of yours," he told Jackson and the other Northern representatives. "You have no right to touch it, still less to demand a reason of us for its continuance."[7]

Francis Thomas of Maryland chimed in with yet another reason for the House to reject the abolitionist petition. "We have been told," he observed, "that great and general excitement has already been produced in some of the southern States, by the circulation of a few fanatical pamphlets. If this be true," he went on, "is it not madness, worse than madness, to struggle to elicit evidence that there is in that House any one man willing to re-echo the sentiment which these incendiary publications contain? I have been opposed, Sir, to any discussion on this subject."[8]

The fight dragged on. Finally, on May 18, 1836, the House adopted, by a vote of 117–68, a resolution that would be known to history as the gag rule. "Whereas it is extremely important and desirable that the agitation of this subject [slavery] should be finally arrested, for the purpose of restoring tranquility to the public mind," the rule said, "petitions, memorials, resolutions, propositions, or papers, relating in any way, or to any extent whatsoever, to the subject of slavery, shall, without exception, be laid upon the table, [and] no further action whatever shall be had thereon."[9] In short, the House of Representatives not only stopped accepting abolitionist petitions but also prohibited its members from discussing such petitions in any way—they were gagged.

Among the gag rule's most forceful opponents was Representative John Quincy Adams, who denounced it as a "direct violation of the Constitution of the United States, the rules of this House, and the rights of my constituents."[10] Adams also recognized a basic principle of political debate that his Southern colleagues had apparently forgotten: namely, the act of suppressing speech only adds more fuel to the speaker's fire. "If you come to the resolution that this House will not receive any more petitions, what will be the consequence?" Adams demanded. "You will have discussion . . . and what will the discussion amount to? A discussion on the merits of slavery." What is more, that discussion would take place in the very heart of the federal government. "Every speech made by a Representative from north of Mason and Dixon's line," Adams warned, "will be an incendiary pamphlet, and what will you do with them? The speeches of my colleagues, probably of myself, will be incendiary."[11]

The petition that Adams now held in his hand on February 6, 1837, "from twenty-two persons, declaring themselves to be slaves," certainly qualified as incendiary in the eyes of his proslavery colleagues. "If the gentleman from Massachusetts intended to present this petition," sputtered Julius Alford of Georgia, Alford himself "should move, as an act of justice to the South . . . that it be taken from the House and burnt."[12] Francis Pickens of South Carolina was prepared to go even further. The petition was evidence of "collusion" between Adams and the slaves, he announced: "It broke down the principle that the slave could only be known through his master. For this [Adams] was indictable, under statute, for aiding and abetting insurrection."[13]

The proslavery contingent also had something else to worry about. A petition from slaves to the federal government assumed that slaves had the right to petition the federal government in the first place. And no representative of a slaveholding state could possibly agree to that. "Are slaves included in the description of the 'people of the United States' in the preamble to the Constitution?" Hopkins Holsey of Georgia asked in incredulity. "The gentleman from Massachusetts, by attempting to introduce such a principle into our legislation, has . . . aimed a deadly blow at the State I have the honor to represent."[14]

If slaves possessed the right to petition—which appeared in the First Amendment, right there at the top of the Bill of Rights—what other constitutional freedoms did they possess? The right to life, liberty, and property? The right to keep and bear arms for self-defense?

If this line of thinking were followed to its logical conclusion, it would fatally undermine the very foundations of the slave system. As Georgia's Waddy Thompson observed, "From the position that slaves have a right to petition to that which should assert their right to vote, 'the step is short and natural.' They can have no such right, unless they have political rights." What is more, Thompson warned, "if they have, to refuse them an agency in making the laws by which those rights are guarded is to violate the great fundamental principle of our Revolution. If they have the right to petition, the principle must be carried out to that extent." Thompson would "not argue such a question for any other purpose," he hastened to add, "than to show the enormity of the act of offering such a petition."[15]

John Quincy Adams was well aware of the enormity of his act. Indeed, that was the whole reason why he was performing the act in the first place. The subject of slavery was often likened to a hornet's nest in those days—a topic better left untouched. Adams was going to give the hornet's nest a series of vigorous kicks.

The kicking commenced on February 9. After sitting quietly for the better part of three days while his Southern colleagues threatened disunion, demanded his censure, and even called for his arrest, Adams requested the privilege of speaking in his own defense before "the resolution of censure was to be passed."[16] The speech that followed was a frontal assault on both the supposed legality of the gag rule and the underlying proslavery sentiment that kept it in place.

Adams opted to come clean about his motives at the outset. "I was anxious that every member of this House should record his vote, for all time to come, on a question of such importance—a question which opened the whole subject of the condition of slaves in this country." Do slaves have the right of petition? That was the question. And the answer, Adams declared, must be an emphatic *yes*. The right of petition is "given, by the God of Nature, to every man when he created him." Furthermore, it is "a right which the framers of our Constitution would have spurned the very idea of abridging or limiting, or restricting to any particular color or class of men!" It is a right "belonging to every human creature," Adams concluded, "which does not depend upon the condition of the petitioner, and which cannot be denied to man in any condition."[17]

It was the familiar, soaring language of the Declaration of Independence. "All Men are created equal," that document famously held, and "are endowed by their Creator with certain unalienable Rights." Because the right of petition was one such right, Adams maintained, slaves enjoyed it to the same absolute degree that free whites enjoyed it. Adams did not go on to say what other inalienable rights slaves might possess by virtue of their humanity, but he really did not need to. The antislavery implications of his dramatic argument were impossible to miss.

In the end, the House of Representatives opted not to formally censure the former president. But a majority of its members did thoroughly reject Adams's position. "This House cannot receive the said petition [from twenty-two slaves] without disregarding its own dignity," declared an official House resolution, passed on February 11 by a vote of 160–35. Another resolution immediately followed, this one adopted by a vote of 162–18: "Slaves do not possess the right of petition secured to the people of the United States by the Constitution."[18]

In theory, the matter was closed. The House would keep on rejecting abolitionist pleas for a number of years to come. Despite his best efforts, Adams had lost the battle over the gag rule and the right of petition. Or at least that is one way of looking at it. Here is another: by daring to kick the hornet's nest, Adams forced the House of Representatives to debate the merits of slavery, something its proslavery members had done everything in their power to prevent. That debate, in turn, received widespread national attention, garnering headlines throughout both the North and the South. For the members of the burgeoning abolitionist movement, it was a galvanizing chain of events. Here was a former president of the United States (and the son of another former president) championing their cause—striking a blow against the slave power—right in the heart of the nation's capital. Inspired by Adams's actions, the abolitionists promptly redoubled their efforts, mailing more antislavery petitions, publishing more antislavery broadsides, giving more antislavery speeches. So, yes, Adams lost the battle. But his exploits undeniably served as a rousing call to arms for the greater war over slavery that was still to come.

Among those who heard the call was a young slave living in nearby Maryland. "I well remember getting possession of a speech by John Quincy Adams, made in Congress about slavery and freedom, and reading it to my fellow slaves," Frederick Douglass later recounted, possibly referring to an 1831 speech by Adams on the subject. "What joy and gladness it produced to know that so great, so good a man was pleading for us, and further, to know that there was a large and growing class of people in the north called abolitionists, who were moving for our freedom."[19]

It should come as no surprise that the long-running controversy over abolitionist petitions to Congress would make such a lasting impression on the mind of Frederick Douglass. In his various speeches on the subject throughout the 1830s, John Quincy Adams, a literal son of the founding fathers, had invoked, again and again, the most basic and venerable principles of American freedom: unalienable rights and constitutional liberty. In the decades to come, Douglass, a self-appointed heir of the founding fathers, would invoke those very same principles in his own remarkable struggle against slavery. In a sense, Douglass picked up where Adams left off. Not only would Douglass become a leader of the abolitionist movement, but he would do so while enlisting both the Declaration of Independence and the Constitution in the antislavery crusade. He would demand that the United States of America finally live up to the promises of liberty and equality that were enshrined in its founding documents.

But before all of that could happen, Frederick Douglass would have to make his escape from slavery.

"The Cruelty and Wickedness of Slavery"

Frederick Augustus Washington Bailey was born into slavery in Tuckahoe, Maryland, in Talbot County, on the state's eastern shore, sometime in February 1818. Like most slaves, he never knew the exact date of his birth. The name Douglass came later, adopted after he had escaped from bondage and was establishing his new life in freedom. He took the name in tribute to James Douglas, a figure in Sir Walter Scott's epic poem, *The Lady of the Lake*. Frederick's mother, a slave named Harriet Bailey, died when he was just seven years old. He barely knew her. "I never saw my mother, to know her as such, more than four or five times in my life," Douglass would later write. She worked twelve miles away, on a different farm, and "made her journeys to see [her son] in the night, traveling the whole distance on foot, after the performance of her day's work. She was a field hand, and a whipping is the penalty of not being in the field at sunrise."[20] His father, a white man, was widely rumored to be either his first master, Aaron Anthony, or some other slaveholder or overseer. Douglass would never learn the man's identity for sure. "Of my father," he wrote in 1881, "I know nothing."[21]

He spent his earliest years in the care of his maternal grandmother, Betsey Bailey. In 1824 he was placed in the care of his mother's cousin, known to him as Aunt Katy, who ran the plantation's kitchen. "One of the first circumstances that opened my eyes to the cruelty and wickedness of slavery," he would later write, "and the heartlessness of my old master, was the refusal of the latter to interpose his authority, to protect and shield a young woman, who had been most cruelly abused and beaten by his overseer." That young woman, still bleeding from the terrible head wound she had received at the drunken overseer's hands, implored Master Anthony for help. Instead, he told her that he "believed she deserved every bit of it" and "if she did not go home instantly, he would himself take the remaining skin from her neck and back."[22] It would not be the last such outrage that Douglass would either witness or experience during his years in bondage.

In 1826 he was sent to Baltimore, to the home of Hugh Auld, whose brother, Thomas, was Aaron Anthony's son-in-law. "My employment," Douglass recalled, "was to run of errands, and to take care of Tommy," the Auld family's two-year-old son, "to prevent his getting in the way of carriages, and to keep him out of harm's way generally."[23] In effect, his job was to serve as part playmate for the boy, part babysitter. It was in this household that young Frederick was to have one of the most formative experiences of his early life.

It happened because he was learning to read. "The frequent hearing of my mistress reading the bible—for she often read aloud when her husband was absent—soon awakened my curiosity in respect to this *mystery* of reading, and roused in me the desire to learn," he recalled. So he asked his mistress, Sophia Auld, to teach him, and she readily agreed to do so. "Mrs. Auld evidently regarded me simply as a child, like any other child," Douglass later observed. "She had not come to regard me as *property*." Once she had taught him the alphabet, Frederick was off and running, able to "spell words of three or four letters."[24] Proud of her teaching, Sophia Auld told her husband about this literary accomplishment. He responded in shock and fury.

Learning to read "would forever unfit [Frederick] for the duties of a slave," Douglass heard Auld berate his wife. "He should know nothing but the will of his master, and learn to obey it." As it happened, this proved to be a very valuable lesson for the young boy to hear, although it did not exactly impart the sort of instruction that Auld might have wanted. "His discourse was the first decidedly antislavery lecture to which it had been my lot to listen," Douglass dryly observed in 1855. "'Very well,' thought I; 'knowledge unfits a child to be a slave.' I instinctively assented to the proposition; and from that moment I understood the direct pathway from slavery to freedom."[25]

At the age of thirteen, young Frederick got his hands on a book that would change his life forever. First published in 1797, *The Columbian Orator* was intended to serve as a sort of dual textbook and self-help manual for aspiring public speakers. Edited by a Massachusetts teacher named Caleb Bingham, it featured a collection of speeches, essays, poems, and fictional works from a wide assortment of figures, including Socrates, Cicero, and George Washington. The book's objective, Bingham wrote in his preface, was to both teach the building blocks of oratory "and diffuse its spirit among the Youth of America."[26] Young Frederick would discover something even greater than that inside the book's pages. As the literary scholars John Stauffer and Henry Louis Gates Jr. have pointed out, "*The Columbian Orator*'s content was surprisingly radical for a self-help book, in the context of the politics of slavery in antebellum America; several of its three dozen or so selections . . . denounced slavery and emphasized that all people are created equal."[27]

Of particular note was a remarkable fictionalized dialogue between an escaped slave and the master who had just recaptured him. "You have been comfortably fed and lodged, not overworked, and attended with the most humane care when you were sick," the master said. So why escape? Why show such ingratitude?

But the slave had a different view of things and quickly turned the tables on his interrogator. "What have you done, what can you do for me," the slave demanded of the master, "that will compensate for the liberty which you have taken away?"

But "I did not take it away," the master faltered in reply. "You were a slave when I fairly purchased."

The slave again demanded, "Did I give my consent to the purchase?"[28]

In the end, the slave's well-reasoned case for freedom and self-ownership simply overpowered the master, who was forced to acknowledge the great crime he had committed. He then promptly freed the slave.

This dialogue "powerfully affected me," Douglass would later write of his thirteen-year-old self, "and I could not help feeling that the day might come, when the well-directed answers made by the slave to the master, in this instance, would find their counterpart in myself."[29]

That day did come. Armed with the alphabet, young Frederick secretly became his own teacher. In time, he was teaching his fellow slaves how to read and write. Eventually, he would teach America itself about the evils of the peculiar institution.

All told, Frederick Douglass would spend the first twenty years of his life in the grip of slavery. Speaking to the American Anti-Slavery Society on May 6, 1845, he reflected on the innumerable horrors he had faced during that period. "I am not from any of those States where the slaves are said to be in their most degraded condition," he observed, "but from Maryland, where Slavery is said to exist in its mildest form; yet I can stand here and relate atrocities which would make your blood boil." He had experienced wanton cruelty, had watched as families, including his own, were ripped apart. "I have seen women stretched up on the limbs of trees, and their bare backs made bloody with the lash." And all of this, he emphasized, was the norm, not the exception. "Slavery makes it necessary for the slaveholder to commit all conceivable outrages upon the miserable slave," Douglass noted. "It is impossible to hold the slaves in bondage without this."[30] Slavery, as Douglass understood all too well, robbed its victims not only of their earnings but of their very humanity, of their control over their own life and limbs. "This body—is it not mine?" Douglass demanded.[31] It was a point that he would drive home to his audiences, time and time again, in the decades to come.

"I Was Now My Own Master"

"Let southern oppressors tremble." So wrote William Lloyd Garrison in the inaugural issue of the *Liberator*, the antislavery publication that would soon help to establish him as one of the most prominent abolitionists in the world. "I will not retreat a single inch," Garrison continued in that January 1, 1831, editorial. "AND I WILL BE HEARD."[32]

Among those who heard Garrison's uncompromising message in the days ahead was Frederick Douglass, who first encountered the *Liberator* in early 1839, shortly after he made his escape from slavery. "From this time I was brought in contact with the mind of William Lloyd Garrison," Douglass recalled. "His paper took its place with me next to the bible."[33]

Douglass had been dreaming of escape since a young age. In 1836 he first determined to give it a try. "The thought, that year after year had passed away, and my best resolutions to run away had failed and faded," he recalled, "was not a matter to be slept over easily; nor did I easily sleep over it."[34] His plan was simple; joined by several others, he would grab a canoe and flee, by cover of darkness, "out into the Chesapeake Bay, and paddle for its head." Assuming they made it that far, the group would then "turn the canoe adrift, and bend [their] steps toward the north star, till [they] reached a free state."[35] Alas, their plot was discovered at the last minute, and the group was briefly jailed. Their betrayer was most likely a fellow slave.

Two years later, Douglass at last made good on his escape. In September 1838 he traveled north by train and by steamer under a false identity to Philadelphia, New York City, and finally to New Bedford, Massachusetts, where he would earn his "first free dollar" on the dockyards loading ships. "I was now my own master," he proclaimed, "a tremendous fact."[36] He got married along the way. Anna Murray was a free black woman who worked as a housekeeper in Baltimore, where the two had first met approximately a year earlier. She joined him in New York City after she got word that he had arrived safely. Her partnership and financial support had been indispensable to the success of his flight. As their daughter, Rosetta Douglass, later recalled, "Having been able to save the greater part of her earnings," Anna Murray "was willing to share with the man she loved that he might gain the freedom he yearned to possess."[37] Together, Frederick and Anna adopted the new last name under which he would soon become world famous.

"Four or five months after reaching New Bedford," Douglass recalled, "there came a young man to me, with a copy of the 'Liberator.'"[38] Douglass signed himself up for a weekly subscription. He also began attending abolitionist meetings around this time and was soon adding his own voice to the mix. By 1841 he was a fixture on the abolitionist lecture circuit, captivating audiences with his gripping firsthand accounts of life under slavery.

What did Douglass find when he first began reading the *Liberator* in early 1839? He might have learned of the grand antislavery meeting held in Boston's Faneuil Hall on January 21, in which "the doors were thrown wide open to the friends of immediate and unconditional emancipation." It was bitterly cold that day, "the mercury ranged several degrees below zero, and there was no fire to warm the immense hall," the *Liberator* reported. "Yet there was no flinching on the part of those in attendance—some three thousand persons, of both sexes."[39] This would have come as welcome and exciting news indeed. Three thousand abolitionists packed inside the famous Faneuil Hall, which had once been the site of so many important public meetings during the American Revolution! Reading that, Douglass would have felt like he was becoming part of something much bigger, and much more important, than anything he had previously known or imagined—a grand campaign on behalf of human freedom. Little did he know that in just a few years' time, he himself would be speaking to such crowds from that very stage.

Douglass might also have learned from the *Liberator* that the Salem Female Anti-Slavery Society had presented William Lloyd Garrison with $100 "as a token of respect." It was a relatively modest sum, around $2,600 in today's money, but it was a clear sign of the high esteem in which Garrison was held in abolitionist circles. "You have stood, as it were, at the forefront of the hottest battle," wrote Harriet Foster, the society's corresponding secretary, "while against you have been directed the deadly weapons of the enemy."[40] That same issue of the *Liberator* also brought the news that "our dearly-beloved brother, Gerrit Smith, has sent to the General Agent of the Liberator, a check for $50.00." "Among the many things, in which the abolitionists of our country should be agreed," Smith wrote in an accompanying note, are that, first, "the Liberator must be sustained" and, second, "its Editor must be kept above want."[41] A wealthy New York landowner, Smith was a friend and patron to many antislavery ventures. In less than a decade, he would be providing crucial support for Douglass's own newspaper, the *North Star*.

While reading those early issues of his new subscription, Douglass might also have had his first encounter with the case for "nonresistance." In a long document published over several issues in January and February 1839, the writer "Pacificus" argued not only that fidelity to Christian principles required a policy of thoroughgoing abolitionism but that it also required a policy of thoroughgoing pacifism. "Did Christ come to suffer and die for his enemies? Or to make them suffer and die for him?" The answer: "He never, by precept or example, taught men to prevent or conquer evildoers by brute force, by physical pains and penalties, by inflicting pain and death on them; but by love, kindness, long-suffering, by suffering and dying ourselves."[42] Garrison, for his part, was in total agreement with such views and frequently championed them in the pages of his paper.

Had Douglass kept on reading, he might also have learned that nonresistance was effectively tantamount to anarchism. "We cannot acknowledge allegiance to any human government," Pacificus declared. "Perhaps no one sentence in the Non-Resistance Declaration has created more sensation, or elicited more comment," Garrison observed in the January 25 issue. "If any man can refute the reasoning and the facts of that essay, we should be glad to see him do it."[43] A few years later, Douglass himself would take up that very challenge, arguing strenuously in favor of the idea that abolitionists can and in fact should take part in the political process. As for Garrison's pacifism, Douglass would come to dismiss it as preposterous in the face of the state-sanctioned outrages perpetrated under the slave system and later under the South's incipient Jim Crow regime. "Yes, let us have peace," Douglass would say, "but let us have liberty, law, and justice first."[44]

Those conflicts still lay in the future, however. For now, Douglass wholeheartedly embraced both Garrison and the growing Garrisonian school of abolitionist thought. "I had not long been a reader of the Liberator, and listener to its editor, before I got a clear apprehension of the principles of the anti-slavery movement," Douglass would say of those early days in Massachusetts. "I united with it from a sense of delight, as well as duty."[45]

"All on Fire"

William Lloyd Garrison was a prickly sort of fellow. By the age of twenty, as one biographer put it, he was "already one-eyed upon any subject that he [treated]"; the biography continued by suggesting, "It is safe to say that he would, at a moment's notice, have delivered a violent judgment upon any subject that aroused his compassion."[46] Garrison loved to lecture almost as much as he hated to listen. Even in the company of his closest friends and allies, he could be obstinate, domineering, exasperating. "Garrison makes an excellent president at a public meeting, where the order of speakers is in some measure arranged, as he has great felicity in introducing and interlocuting remarks," observed one abolitionist colleague. "But at a meeting for debate he does not answer so well, as he is rather too apt, with all the innocence and simplicity in the world, to do all the talking himself."[47]

He was born in 1805 in Newburyport, Massachusetts. At the age of twelve he became a printer's apprentice. He would spend the remainder of his working life surrounded by the ink-stained tools of the trade. Oliver Johnson, editor of Ohio's *Anti-Slavery Bugle*, among other publications, offered this vivid memory of watching Garrison at work: "The dingy walls; the small windows, bespattered with printer's ink; the press standing in one corner; the long editorial and mailing table, covered with newspapers; the bed of the editor and publisher on the floor; all these make a picture never to be forgotten."[48]

In 1831 Garrison launched the *Liberator*. The inaugural issue made plain that Garrison intended to be a force to be reckoned with. "I am aware, that many object to the severity of my language," he wrote. "But is there no cause for severity? I *will be* as harsh as truth, and as uncompromising as justice. On this subject I do not wish to think, or speak, or write, with moderation. No! No!"[49] The subject he was referring to, of course, was slavery.

The abolitionist Samuel J. May once asked Garrison to soften his approach—to tone it down, as we might say today—fearing that "he was damaging the cause he had so much at heart by the undue severity of his style." "My friend," May said to Garrison, "do try to moderate your indignation, and keep more cool; why, you are all on fire." Garrison took a moment before responding. "Brother May," he declared, "I have need to be *all on fire*, for I have mountains of ice about me to melt." Looking back in 1869 on that exchange, May confessed that he never again "said a word to Mr. Garrison, in complaint of his style," admitting that "I am more than half satisfied now that he was right then, and we who had objected were mistaken."[50]

Garrison sparked controversy right away. The *Liberator* had not even celebrated its first birthday, for example, before the legislature of slaveholding Georgia offered a $5,000 bounty in 1831 "to be paid by the Governor to any person or persons arresting and bringing to trial, under the laws of the State, and prosecuting to conviction, the editor or publisher of 'the Liberator,' or any other person who shall utter, publish, or circulate said paper in Georgia."[51] What crime had the said paper and its editor supposedly committed? As far as the authorities in Georgia were concerned, the writings of Garrison and his fellow abolitionists were designed to stir up the slaves and incite them to revolt. "A price set upon the head of a citizen of Massachusetts—for what?" Garrison retorted. "For daring to give his opinions of the moral aspect of slavery!" Rest assured, he warned his Georgian foes, "the *Liberator* shall yet live—live to warn you of your danger and guilt."[52]

Frederick Douglass took to Garrison's uncompromising style immediately. The *Liberator* and its editor "detested slavery—exposed hypocrisy and wickedness in high places—made no truce with the traffickers in the bodies and souls of men." It was a paper, Douglass declared, "after my own heart."[53]

When the two men finally met in person, at an antislavery convention in Nantucket, Massachusetts, in August 1841, the admiration proved instantly mutual. "I shall never forget his first speech at the convention—the extraordinary emotion it excited in my own mind—the powerful impression it created upon a crowded auditory," Garrison wrote.[54] "I could not help thinking how incomparably superior was this 'chattel,' in all the great qualities of the soul, to any warrior whose deeds are recorded on the page of history."[55]

Together they began barnstorming against slavery, speaking to crowds large and small on behalf of the Massachusetts Anti-Slavery Society (which Garrison helped organize in 1835) and the American Anti-Slavery Society (which Garrison helped organize in 1833). Their combined rhetoric frequently had an electrifying effect on audiences. Douglass often went first, especially in the early days of their work together, offering a vivid and unforgettable firsthand account of the horrors he had experienced during his years in bondage. "When the young man [Douglass] closed late in the evening," one abolitionist reported after witnessing them speak at an 1841 meeting, "Mr. Garrison rose to make the concluding address." Garrison asked the crowd a simple question: "Have we been listening to a thing, a piece of property, or to a man?" The crowd of five hundred roared its answer: "A man! A man!" As the witness concluded, "I think [Garrison] never before nor afterwards felt more profoundly the sacredness of his mission."[56]

Of course, the audiences were not always so receptive to the abolitionist message. Things started off well enough at an appearance in Harrisburg, Pennsylvania, Garrison reported in an 1847 letter to his wife. "I first addressed the meeting, and was listened to, not only without molestation, but with marked attention and respect, though my remarks were stringent, and my accusations severe." But the crowd turned ugly as soon as Douglass rose to speak. "The spirit of rowdyism began to show itself," Garrison wrote, with some understatement. "They came equipped with rotten eggs and brickbats, firecrackers, and other missiles, and made use of them freely."[57] There would be times when Douglass and Garrison had to duck out the back to avoid an angry mob. There would also be times when Douglass had to practically punch his way out.

"An Agreement with Hell"

The core tenets of Garrisonian abolitionism were basically set by the early 1840s. First and foremost was the principle of immediate and unconditional emancipation. Slavery must be abolished today, not tomorrow; it must be abolished now, not later. There was also the principle of nonresistance, which in practice amounted to a religious doctrine of pacifism and nonparticipation in the political system; this included a strict policy of nonvoting and a refusal to join or support any political party. And then there was the related matter of the U.S. Constitution. Writing in the *Liberator* on December 29, 1832, Garrison set the pace. The Constitution, *"dripping as it is with human blood,"* he declared, was the most "heaven-daring arrangement ever made by men for the continuance and protection of a system of the most atrocious villainy ever exhibited on earth." Garrison knew perfectly well that he was now treading on dangerous rhetorical ground. "It is said that if you agitate this question, you will divide the Union," he wrote. Well, bring it on. "We say it is not worth a price like this."[58]

As far as Garrison was concerned, the Constitution was a fundamentally proslavery document, the product of a foul bargain made in 1787 between the free North and the slaveholding South. He would have no part of it; nor would he have any part of the flawed federal union that it had created. Indeed, he thought the Union should be broken up, and he actively encouraged the Northern states to secede.

Even among radical abolitionists, this was a controversial stance. "I am in favor of dissolution if we cannot have abolition," one abolitionist wrote. "But I could wish to see all reasonable means used of reforming before we destroy the Constitution."[59]

Garrison was not so big on "reasonable means." He meant to end American slavery by destroying the very nation-state that he judged guilty of keeping the institution in place. Attacks on the Constitution thus became a regular feature of Garrison's work, appearing routinely in his editorials, speeches, and letters. At the same time, Garrison began lobbying the organized abolitionist movement to formally embrace his views on the subject. Those efforts eventually bore fruit. "The compact which exists between the North and South is 'a covenant with death and an agreement with hell'—involving both parties in atrocious criminality—and should be immediately annulled," announced an 1843 resolution of the Massachusetts Anti-Slavery Society.[60] The resolution had been drafted by Garrison. "We dissolved the Union by a handsome vote," remarked one participant, "after a warm debate."[61]

The New England Anti-Slavery Society followed suit a year later. "The question of the duty of withdrawing from the support of the U.S. Government on account of its pro-slavery character, and of making the dissolution of the Union our main measure, was *the* question of the convention," wrote the abolitionist Edmund Quincy. "The vote surprised us all. At one time we thought it might not pass. . . . But when the roll was called, it seemed as if there were no 'nays' at all."[62] The American Anti-Slavery Society did the same thing that same year. "The principal things we did" at the annual meeting, reported the abolitionist Francis Jackson, "were to mend up the Constitution of our Society, and do what we could to break down the Constitution of the Union."[63] Writing in the *Liberator* on May 31, 1844, Garrison deftly summarized the new Garrisonian consensus. "Until slavery be abolished," he wrote, "the watch word, the rallying-cry, the motto on the banner of the American Anti-Slavery Society shall be, NO UNION WITH SLAVEHOLDERS!"[64]

Next to Garrison himself, perhaps the greatest advocate of the Garrisonian view of the Constitution was Garrison's most trusted and effective lieutenant. Wendell Phillips was born in 1811 to one of the oldest and most distinguished families in Boston. A child of wealth and privilege, he attended the best schools of the day, including Harvard, where he studied constitutional law under Supreme Court justice Joseph Story. "When Beacon Street turned its back on him for joining the abolitionists," observed the historian Richard Hofstadter, "Phillips could indulge in the snobbery of calling his detractors 'men of no family.'"[65] Phillips's original plan had been to follow in the respectable footsteps of his father and become a lawyer. But then he "grew honest," as he later put it, and made it his business "to forward the abolition of slavery." He then stated, "I hold that the world is wrong side up and maintain the propriety of turning it upside down. I go for Disunion and have long since abjured that contemptible mockery, the Constitution of the United States."[66]

Take a close look at the Constitution, Phillips would urge his readers and listeners, and you will find clear evidence of its proslavery character. Start with Article I, Section 2, the notorious Three-Fifths Clause, which said that for purposes of taxation and political representation, state populations "shall be determined by adding to the whole Number of free Persons, including those bound to Service for a Term of Years, and excluding Indians not taxed, three fifths of all other Persons." This clause "confers on a slaveholding community additional political power for every slave held among them," Phillips argued, "and thus tempts them to continue to uphold the system."[67]

Turn next to Article I, Section 9, which dealt with congressional authority over the foreign slave trade. It read as follows: "The Migration or Importation of such Persons as any of the States now existing shall think proper to admit, shall not be prohibited by the Congress prior to the year one thousand eight hundred and eight." This clause "disgraces the nation," Phillips declared, "by a pledge not to abolish that traffic [in human slaves] till after twenty years, *without obliging Congress to do so even then.*"[68]

And do not forget Article IV, Section 2, better known as the Fugitive Slave Clause, which stated that "no Person, held to Service or Labour in one State, under the Laws thereof, escaping into another, shall, in Consequence of any Law or Regulation therein, be discharged from such Service or Labour; but shall be delivered up on Claim of the Party to whom such Service or Labour may be due." This clause, Phillips averred, was nothing less than "a promise on the part of the whole nation to return fugitive slaves to their masters, a deed which God's law expressly condemns, and which every noble feeling of our nature repudiates with loathing and contempt."[69]

Phillips would also point his accusing finger at two additional constitutional provisions. Article I, Section 8, granted Congress the authority to "suppress Insurrections." Article IV, Section 4, meanwhile, said that the federal government would protect each state "against domestic Violence." These clauses, Phillips argued, "perfectly innocent in themselves, yet being made with the fact directly in view that slavery exists among us, do deliberately pledge the whole national force against the unhappy slave if he imitate our fathers and resist oppression." For Phillips, such evidence was irrefutable, and the case was closed. Such is "the guilt and infamy of this national bargain," he concluded, and "the duty of each individual to trample it under his feet."[70]

"The Case of Our Slaves"

Garrison and Phillips were correct about the proslavery intentions of certain founding fathers. A number of slaveholders took part in the framing of the Constitution, and the final document bore certain hallmarks of their influence and handiwork. What is more, some of the Constitution's most prominent framers openly acknowledged the document's entanglements with slavery. For instance, consider the national debate over ratification. Between October 1787 and May 1788, Alexander Hamilton, James Madison, and John Jay authored a series of eighty-five essays now collectively known as *The Federalist Papers*. Published anonymously in newspapers and pamphlets under the pseudonym Publius, these writings represent one of the earliest sustained efforts to explain the meaning of the Constitution, which was then being considered by the states.

Slavery is mentioned several times in *The Federalist Papers*. In *Federalist 42*, for example, Madison explained that among the powers "lodged in the general government" was "a power to prohibit, after the year 1808, the importation of slaves."[71] Meanwhile, in *Federalist* 54, Madison explained that the Three-Fifths Clause was crafted precisely to deal with the issue of slavery. "The federal constitution," he wrote, "decides with great propriety on the case of our slaves, when it views them in the mixt character of persons and property." The fact is, Madison explained, that slaves "partake of both these qualities; being considered by our laws, in some respects, as persons, and in other respects as property." Furthermore, "it is admitted that if the laws were to restore the rights which have been taken away, the negroes could no longer be refused an equal share of representation with the other inhabitants."[72]

In short, not only was the Constitution intended to include several references to the institution of slavery, but thanks to the publication and circulation of *The Federalist Papers*, the ratifying public was made well aware of that fact.

"I Could Not Always Obey"

For the first decade of his career as an abolitionist, Frederick Douglass was, in his own words, "a faithful disciple of William Lloyd Garrison, and fully committed to his doctrine touching the pro-slavery character of the Constitution."[73] His speeches and writings on the subject during this period, including his private letters, closely followed the Garrisonian line. In March 1847, for example, Douglass capped off a nearly two-year tour of England, Ireland, and Scotland with a rousing speech to over a thousand abolitionists and antislavery sympathizers in London. The prospect of returning to the land of his birth, he told the crowd, brought him no joy at all. "The fact is, the whole system, the entire network of American society, is one great falsehood, from beginning to end." Just look at the U.S. Constitution, he said, "over the very gateway of which [the founders] inscribed, 'to secure the blessings of liberty.'" Yet that very same document contained "no less than three clauses" giving aid and comfort to slavery. The provision providing against "domestic insurrection," he said, "converts every white American into an enemy to the black man." The Fugitive Slave Clause "consecrates every rood of earth in that land over which the star-spangled banner waves as slave-hunting ground."[74] Oh no, Douglass declared, "I really cannot be very patriotic when speaking of their national institutions and boasted constitution."[75]

He made a similar point before a capacity crowd in Syracuse, New York. "The Constitution I hold to be a radically and essentially slaveholding document," Douglass declared. "For my part I had rather that my right hand should wither by my side than cast a ballot under the Constitution of the United States."[76] In a letter to Thomas Van Rensselaer, a former slave who was then editing the abolitionist New York City paper the *Ram's Horn*, Douglass summarized his then-Garrisonian stance in a nutshell. "The foundation of this government—the great Constitution itself," he wrote, "is nothing more than a compromise with man-stealers."[77]

Yet despite such professions of fidelity and agreement, certain rifts were starting to develop between Douglass and the Garrisonians. Douglass "was growing, and needed room," as he later put it, and he increasingly found himself chafing under the paternalistic guidance of Garrison and other allies. "Give us the facts," one abolitionist leader told him. "We will take care of the philosophy." In other words, *your job is to serve as a sort of walking exhibit against slavery, while our job is to provide the intellectual arguments that cinch the case.* What is worse, some of those same abolitionists told Douglass, one of the most eloquent public speakers of the day, to dumb it down in order to give a more convincing performance. "It was said to me, 'Better have a *little* of the plantation manner of speech than not,'" he recalled. But as Douglass explained, "I could not always obey, for I was now reading and thinking. It did not entirely satisfy me to *narrate* wrongs; I felt like *denouncing* them."[78] It would not be the last time that he rejected the misguided advice of his ostensible allies.

More fundamental disagreements were also taking shape. For one thing, Douglass was never destined to be much of a pacifist. According to Garrison, abolitionist principles "lead us to reject, and to entreat the oppressed to reject, the use of all carnal weapons for deliverance from bondage." Emancipation must be brought about via moral suasion, Garrison maintained, via "the opposition

of moral purity to moral corruption."[79] In short, preach human freedom, change hearts and minds, and the end of slavery will follow.

Douglass was all for preaching antislavery, but he was not so keen
on turning the other cheek. This became abundantly clear with the
publication of his 1845 book, *Narrative of the Life of Frederick Douglass, an American Slave*, the first of the three autobiographies that he
would write. In one of the book's most celebrated passages, Douglass described how an act of violent resistance on his part became
"the turning point in my career as a slave."[80] It happened when he
was fifteen years old. After living for seven years in the Baltimore
home of Hugh Auld, Douglass was sent back to rural Talbot County
in 1832, when he fell under the control of Hugh's brother, Thomas
Auld (the son-in-law of Frederick's first master, Aaron Anthony).
Master Thomas quickly "found me unsuitable to his purposes,"[81] as
Douglass put it. Among other infractions, the teenage slave kept let-
ting Auld's horse escape. The reason "for this kind of carelessness,
or carefulness," Douglass later winked, "was that I could always get
something to eat" at a nearby farm while out retrieving the animal.[82]
Douglass was repeatedly flogged for such offenses. Eventually, Auld
decided that a more extreme brand of punishment was called for.

In January 1833 Auld sent Douglass to work as a field hand a dozen
miles away under the supervision of a farmer named Edward Covey,
who, as Douglass put it, "enjoyed the most unbounded reputation
for being a first-rate overseer and negro-breaker."[83] Covey ran a sort
of side business that involved taking on troublesome slaves for a year
or so and bending them to his will. Under this arrangement, Covey
reaped the benefits of short-term forced labor while the slaveholders later benefitted from the "improved" slaves that he sent back to
them. The job suited Covey well; he was equipped with both a violent temper and a devious mind. Among the slaves he was known as
the Snake, a nickname earned by Covey's practice of sneaking up on
them while they were working in the field, in the hopes of catching
them relaxing so that he might deliver a savage beating.

The first six months that Douglass spent under Covey's authority were basically a form of hell on earth. He was savagely whipped
for even the smallest of offenses. He was punched and kicked and

had his head gashed open by a blow from a hickory slat. Before long, Douglass was succumbing to the dehumanizing effects of such monstrous treatment. He lost his desire to read, even to think. It was soul crushing. "The dark night of slavery closed in upon me," Douglass wrote of that experience. "Behold a man transformed into a brute."[84]

Douglass reached his limit one day in August. Covey had ambushed him in the stables, attempting to bind his feet with a rope and deliver yet another beating for a supposed infraction. Except this time Douglass fought back. He grabbed Covey by the throat and tightened his grip, "causing the blood to run where I touched him with the ends of my fingers."[85] They hit the ground together in a tangle, rolling and thrashing and jockeying for control. Their fight lasted for almost two hours until Covey, puffing with exhaustion, at last gave up and backed away. After that, their relationship underwent a permanent transformation. Douglass would spend another six months in Covey's presence, yet the much-feared "breaker" never again dared to raise a hand against him. For Douglass, it was both a physical triumph and something much greater still. The victory had revived his human spirt and reawakened his desire to escape to freedom. "He only can understand the deep satisfaction which I experienced," Douglass wrote, "who has himself repelled by force the bloody arm of slavery."[86] This was hand-to-hand combat with profound moral implications.

Douglass also began to speak favorably in public about organized slave revolts. He was particularly inspired by the actions of a slave named Madison Washington. On October 25, 1841, the slave ship *Creole* left Richmond, Virginia, carrying 135 slaves, bound for New Orleans, Louisiana. On November 7, nineteen of those slaves, led by Madison Washington, rose up against the crew and took control of the ship. Two days later, they arrived at Nassau, the capital of the Bahamas, which was then a British colony. The mutineers appealed to the local British authorities to recognize their freedom. Because Britain had abolished the foreign slave trade in 1807, that recognition was ultimately granted. All told, the uprising liberated 133 people, while claiming the lives of just three (one crew member and two slaves). Numerically speaking, that made it one of the most successful slave revolts in American history.

Abolitionists divided bitterly over whether or not such violent tactics should be encouraged among the enslaved. Among those in favor of encouraging slave revolts was the abolitionist Henry Highland Garnet, pastor of the Liberty Street Negro Presbyterian Church in Troy, New York, who praised Madison Washington, "that bright star of freedom," as a prime example of why black Americans must stand up and fight. "Let your motto be RESISTANCE! RESISTANCE! RESISTANCE!" Garnet declared in an 1843 speech before the National Convention of Colored Citizens in Buffalo. "No oppressed people have ever secured their liberty without resistance."[87]

The Garrisonians took the opposite view. "We say emphatically to the man of color, trust not the counsels that lead you to the shedding of blood," the *Liberator* responded to Garnet's speech. "We fervently hope that Mr. Garnet had no other or further intentions, than merely to write what he thought a high-sounding address. We would fain hope that he would be shocked to find his counsels taking effect."[88]

Douglass was present that day in Buffalo and heard Garnet's speech for himself. In the immediate aftermath, he added his voice to the chorus of Garrisonian disapproval, complaining of "too much physical force both in the address and remarks of Garnet."[89] But Douglass soon began singing a different tune. Madison Washington "has made some noise in the world with that act of his," Douglass observed in an 1845 speech. "Inspired with the love of freedom, with the determination to get it or die in the attempt," the slave leader had thrown off not only his own shackles but those of more than one hundred others.[90] That made him a hero.

Douglass also heaped scorn on those hypocritical white Americans, whose own nation was founded on revolutionary principles yet who objected to the sight of black Americans fighting for their own rights. "Our Congress," Douglass remarked, "was thrown into an uproar that *Madison Washington* had in imitation of *George Washington* gained liberty."[91] Speaking in London two years later, Douglass would celebrate "the noble Madison Washington, who broke his fetters on the deck of the Creole."[92]

The *Creole* revolt also inspired Douglass to try his hand at writing fiction. *The Heroic Slave*, which first appeared in 1853, is a novella-length portrait of Madison Washington written by Douglass in a semijournalistic third-person style. It told the story of Washington's deeds by drawing on several fictionalized perspectives, including that of the "first mate" on the *Creole*. "I confess, gentlemen, I felt myself in the presence of a superior man; one who, had he been a white man, I would have followed willingly and gladly in any honorable enterprise," the fictionalized sailor told a barroom audience, several months after the revolt at sea. "Our difference of color was the only ground for difference of action. It was not that his principles were wrong in the abstract; for they are the principles of 1776."[93]

Alert readers have long noticed that Douglass's imagined version of Madison Washington just happened to bear a strong resemblance to Douglass himself. Washington "was of manly form," according to *The Heroic Slave*, and "his voice, that unfailing index of the soul, though full and melodious, had that in it which could terrify as well as charm."[94] This arresting work of literature left no doubt that its author now fully supported violent resistance against slavery and that he did so on both moral and practical grounds. Indeed, Douglass would go on to endorse violent resistance on many more occasions in the years to come. He declared in 1854, "The True Remedy for the Fugitive Slave Bill is a good revolver, a steady hand, and a determination to shoot down any man attempting to kidnap."[95] To say the least, this was a far cry from Garrison's belief that the oppressed should reject "all carnal weapons for deliverance from bondage."[96]

"Meeting Opposite Views"

There was also trouble brewing between Douglass and Garrison on the journalism front. By 1847 Douglass had his eyes on a new enterprise and was preparing to strike out on his own. "A tolerably well-conducted press in the hands of persons of [my] despised race," Douglass thought, would "prove a most powerful means of removing prejudice." Yet at that time, "there was not, in the United States, a single newspaper regularly published by the colored people."[97] Douglass planned to do something about that and had already raised around $2,000 from British admirers to cover the costs of a printing press and other necessary materials. After proving himself as an orator and as an author, Douglass was eager to make his mark as an editor.

But Garrison strongly opposed the venture, arguing that another abolitionist publication was not necessary and that the editorial duties would keep Douglass off the lecture circuit, where, Garrison maintained, Douglass's talents were needed the most. "It would be no gain, but rather a loss, to the anti-slavery cause, to have him withdrawn to any considerable extent from the work of popular agitation," Garrison wrote. Besides, "it is quite impractical to combine the editor with the lecturer, without either causing the paper to be more or less neglected, or the sphere of lecturing to be seriously circumscribed."[98] That last point was certainly open to debate. As the historian Philip Foner once remarked, "Douglass could have replied (as did some Abolitionists critical of Garrison's reasoning) that the editor of the *Liberator* seemed to be capable of combining lecturing and editorial duties."[99]

Garrison may also have been put off by his star pupil's growing independence. In a letter to his wife, Garrison would complain that Douglass never "asked my advice in any particular whatever" about the newspaper project. "Such conduct grieves me to the heart."[100] As sometimes happens in such relationships, the student was starting to eclipse the teacher.

Douglass was certainly willing to listen to the critical views of his allies, but he was not about to wait around for their permission. He did, however, make one notable concession. "From motives of peace, instead of issuing my paper in Boston, among New England friends," he explained, he relocated to Rochester, New York, "where the local circulation of my paper—'THE NORTH STAR'—would not interfere with that of the *Liberator*."[101] The move paid off. Within a few years, Douglass was able to report that the *North Star* "sustains itself, and partly sustains my large family."[102] What is more, ensconced in his new editorial roost, Douglass quickly began establishing himself as one of the most singular and influential journalistic voices in the growing national debate over slavery. "The slave holder is the every day robber of the slave, of his birthright to liberty, property, and the pursuit of happiness," Douglass wrote in the paper's first issue, published on December 3, 1847. The slave's "right to be free is unquestionable—the wrong to enslave him is self evident—the duty to emancipate him is imperative."[103] Even his proslavery opponents were forced to concede that Douglass was a potent writer. In today's parlance, the *North Star* became a must read.

The move to New York also paid off in another, more unexpected way. In those days, upstate New York was a hotbed of the so-called political abolitionists, the non-Garrisonian faction who maintained that antislavery activists should vote, should run for office, and should otherwise use the political process to advance the cause. They were also famous for arguing that the Constitution was chock full of antislavery principles that should be used aggressively in the fight against human bondage. The Liberty Party, founded by political abolitionists in Warsaw, New York, in 1840, was the direct product of such thinking and served as a principal vector for the spread of such ideas. The Liberty Party declared in an official resolution at its 1848 national convention in Buffalo, "Slavery—the crime of crimes—cannot be legalized."[104]

It was in this new environment, removed from the immediate reach of the Garrisonians while nestled among Liberty Party stalwarts, in which Douglass first began to entertain doubts about the wisdom of Garrison's uncompromising stance on slavery and the Constitution. Within four years of his arrival in Rochester, Douglass's thinking on the subject would undergo a radical transformation. "But for the responsibility of conducting a public journal, and the necessity imposed upon me of meeting opposite views from abolitionists in this state," Douglass wrote of his early years in Rochester, "I should in all probability have remained as firm in my disunion views as any other disciple of William Lloyd Garrison."[105]

Frederick Douglass did not yet realize it at the time, but he was about to embark on an intellectual quest that would divide the abolitionist movement and reshape the national debate over slavery and the Constitution.

2

"An Anti-slavery Instrument"

On September 20, 1837, Alvan Stewart, the president and founder of the New York Anti-Slavery Society, delivered a speech at his group's annual meeting in the city of Utica. His topic, "A Constitutional Argument on the Subject of Slavery," undoubtedly led some members of the audience to expect to hear a version of William Lloyd Garrison's famous position on the subject—namely, that all right-thinking abolitionists must reject the Constitution as a diabolical compact drenched in human blood. But Stewart, a lawyer by training, had a very different sort of case to present that day.

According to the terms of the Fifth Amendment to the Constitution, Stewart observed, "No Person shall be . . . deprived of life, liberty, or property, without due process of law." And what is due process of law? It is a thoroughgoing proceeding, he explained, one that involves "an indictment or presentment by a grand jury, of not less than twelve, nor more than twenty-three men; a trial by a petit jury of twelve men, and a judgement pronounced on the finding of a jury, by a court."[1]

Now consider the supposedly lawful institution of slavery. Has a single slave anywhere in the United States of America, Stewart asked, received anything that even remotely approximates due process? Has any slave been indicted by a grand jury? Gone to trial before a jury of twelve? Received the judgment of a court? No, of course not. Yet the Fifth Amendment requires nothing less than "indictment, trial, and judgment against a person as a slave," if that person is going to be lawfully deprived of liberty. "Without this commission, this constitutional authority, growing out of an indictment, trial, and judgment against the slave," Stewart argued, "the act of the master, in exercising dominion over the slave, is as unconstitutional as for a man, without commission, election, or appointment, to assume the duties of sheriff, and hang a man, untried, but suspected of murder."[2] In other words, slavery, as it then existed in the United States, was occurring in open violation of the Fifth Amendment.

To be sure, Stewart observed, there will be those who object to this argument on the grounds that slaves have never been entitled to any rights under the Fifth Amendment. But who, he asked, can deny that slaves count as "persons" for constitutional purposes? Does not the Three-Fifths Clause refer to slaves as "other persons" when calculating state populations? Does not the Fugitive Slave Clause speak of the slave as a "person, held to Service or Labour?" Surely, "after having previously twice used the word 'person' where it meant slaves," he said, "if it did not intend to embrace the slave, there would have been an exception in relation to the slave." Yet there was no exception in the language of the Fifth Amendment, which unequivocally stated that "no Person" shall be denied due process. "Every human being in this Union, black or white, bond or free," therefore, "has invaluable blessings secured to him by" this constitutional provision.[3]

What this argument meant in practice, Stewart continued, is that any supposed slave, "before they shall be deprived of their liberty, shall always have an opportunity, as ample as the benignity of the common law, to vindicate their freedom." In short, each and every slave is entitled to receive his or her day in court. What is more, "if the master could not produce a record of conviction, by which the particular slave had been deprived of his liberty, by indictment, trial, and judgment at a court, the judge would be obligated under the oath which he must have taken, to obey the Constitution of his country, to discharge the slave and give him his full liberty."[4]

The name Alvan Stewart is mostly forgotten today, even among historians who specialize in nineteenth-century America. That is too bad. Because on that day in 1837, speaking to an audience of several hundred people in upstate New York, Stewart made abolitionist history. With his close reading and adroit application of the Fifth Amendment to the problem of slavery, Stewart presented the first comprehensive abolitionist argument in favor of an antislavery interpretation of the Constitution.

Fortunately for the abolitionist movement, it would not be the last such argument. Indeed, the cause of antislavery constitutionalism was just about to enter its golden age. In 1845 a radical lawyer named Lysander Spooner published a book called *The Unconstitutionality of Slavery*. According to this influential work, the Constitution "not only does not recognize or sanction slavery, as a legal institution, but . . . on the contrary, it presumes all men to be free."[5] That same year, William Goodell, a founder of the abolitionist Liberty Party and a veteran antislavery journalist, published a revised edition of his book *Views of American Constitutional Law, in Its Bearing upon American Slavery*. "Do we live under a free government, or a despotism?" Goodell wrote. Does the Constitution "'secure the blessings of liberty' to its founders and their 'posterity,'" as the document famously states in its preamble, "or does it guaranty the curses of slavery to large and increasing numbers of them, and ensure the ultimate wreck of the whole nation's freedom?"[6] In answer, Goodell placed the Constitution squarely on the side of liberty and free government.

And then there was Gerrit Smith, the wealthy philanthropist and tireless antislavery activist. Like Goodell, Smith, too, was a founder of the Liberty Party. He was also the party's presidential candidate in the elections of 1848 and 1856 (Smith ran for president again in 1860 on the Radical Abolitionist ticket). "The Federal Constitution," Smith declared at the state Liberty Party Convention at Cazenovia, New York, on July 3, 1849, "clearly requires the abolition of every part of American slavery." At that same convention, Smith also threw down the gauntlet before the followers of William Lloyd Garrison. "The Phillipses, and Quinceys, and Garrisons, and Douglasses, who throw away this staff of anti-slavery accomplishment, and chime in with the popular cry, that the Constitution is pro-slavery," Smith announced, "do, thereby, notwithstanding their anti-slavery hearts, make themselves practically and effectively pro-slavery."[7]

Those were fighting words. Yet the funny thing was, Frederick Douglass was starting to think the same thing about both himself and his Garrisonian allies. Douglass had recently begun his own course of study in constitutional history and theory, and his findings were beginning to spark doubts about Garrison's position. "Garrison sees in the Constitution precisely what John C. Calhoun sees there," Douglass would write in 1850.[8] Perhaps both of them were wrong. Perhaps the Constitution might stand for something else. For several years, Douglass pored over the Constitution's text and meaning. At the same time, in both his public writings and his private letters, he grappled with the competing interpretations offered by Garrison and Smith. Writing in the *North Star* on May 15, 1851, Douglass finally announced the results of all his research and thinking. After "a careful study of the writings of Lysander Spooner, of Gerrit Smith, and of William Goodell," Douglass wrote, he had changed his mind and now believed that the Constitution should be "wielded in behalf of emancipation."[9]

It was a momentous and far-reaching decision. Douglass, who had once been Garrison's star pupil and protégé, would now break definitively with his former mentor. At the same time, a pivotal new chapter in Douglass's life would open up. He would soon become a potent force in the field of electoral politics. The antislavery movement would never be the same again.

To understand how Douglass's remarkable intellectual transformation came about, we must first understand the origins of that transformation in the tumultuous world of the constitutional abolitionists.

"Holy Courage"

Gerrit Smith became a radical abolitionist practically overnight. He was born in 1797 in Utica, New York, to one of the largest landholding families in the state. He became interested in antislavery principles at a young age, though his energies were first directed in favor of the American Colonization Society, which maintained that the solution to the problem of slavery was to resettle black Americans en masse somewhere in Africa. Like most supporters of colonization, Smith kept his distance from the full-throated abolitionists.

But then everything changed for Smith on October 21, 1835. On that day, some six hundred abolitionist delegates arrived in Utica for an antislavery convention. Those delegates were not warmly received. Their meeting, held at the courthouse, was surrounded by a riotous proslavery mob, which pounded on the doors and eventually forced its way inside. The mob proceeded to break up the gathering, shouting down speakers and menacing delegates with threats of violence. "I am ready to tear the rascals to pieces," one proslavery thug was heard to shout. The mob's passions had been inflamed over the course of several preceding days by a number of antiabolitionist speeches and meetings held in protest of the pending convention. One of the fiercest voices raised against the abolitionists was that of local congressman Samuel Beardsley, who represented the surrounding district in the nation's capital. "The disgrace of having an Abolition Convention held in the city is a deeper one than that of twenty mobs," Beardsley declared. "It would be better to have Utica razed to its foundations, or to have it destroyed like Sodom and Gomorrah, than to have the Convention meet here."[10] The congressman got his wish. The convention was literally run out of town.

Among those present that day in Utica was Gerrit Smith, who lived about thirty miles away in the village of Peterboro. He did not attend as a delegate. Rather, he came merely as an interested local citizen with antislavery sympathies. But the mob assault drew Smith from the sidelines and placed him squarely on the field. Amid the shouting and cursing inside the Utica courthouse, Smith raised his own voice to invite every delegate back to Peterboro, where he promised that they could meet and speak freely. The next day, several hundred people arrived to take him up on the offer. This time around, the convention went on without a hitch.

Smith did not just play host in Peterboro. He also delivered the most memorable address of the day, a rousing defense of both free speech in general and the right to speak out against slavery in particular. "I knew before that slavery would not survive free discussion," Smith told the crowd. "But the demands recently put forth [by the proslavery forces] for our surrender of the right of discussion, and the avowed reasons of that demand, involve a full concession of this fact, that free discussion is incompatible with slavery." Just ask yourselves, he said, "for what purpose are we called to throw down our pens, and seal up our lips, and sacrifice our influence over our fellow-men?" The answer: "That one sixth of our American people may never know their rights; that two and a half millions of our countrymen, crushed in the cruel folds of slavery, may remain in all their misery and despair, without pity and without hope."[11] Given the stakes, he argued, the abolitionist movement must never allow itself to be silenced.

It was a turning point in Smith's life. From that day forward, he would be a committed radical in the cause of human freedom. Confiding in his journal a few days after the mob attack and resulting Peterboro convention, Smith penned a few words intended to shore himself up for the arduous new course on which he was set. "The Lord carry much instruction to my mind and heart from the scenes of the past week," he wrote, "and may He teach me, and enable me to rely on Himself for protection in all the perils that surround and threaten me. The Lord inspire my heart with holy courage."[12]

"To Give Up the Constitution Is to Give Up the Slave"

Gerrit Smith went to war against slavery on multiple fronts. In the words of one biographer, "Letters were ceaselessly flowing from his pen; speeches poured steadily from his lips; money streamed in full current from his purse."[13] He rarely missed the chance to preach or promote abolitionist ideas. And one of the ideas that was nearest and dearest to his heart was that of an abolitionist Constitution. "The constitution is an anti-slavery instrument, and needs but to be administered in consistency with its principles to effectuate the speedy overthrow of the whole system of American slavery," Smith wrote to the poet, editor, and fellow abolitionist John Greenleaf Whittier in 1844. Yet thanks to those misguided souls who viewed the Constitution as proslavery, "this shield which God has given us to put over the head of the slave we have traitorously made the protection of the slaveholder."[14]

Speaking in Albany, New York, in 1850, Smith maintained that the only reason why the institution of slavery was still standing was because the slaveholder had been allowed to "plead law for his matchless crime. But take from him that plea, and he will be too weak to continue his grasp upon his victims." Indeed, Smith declared, "let the North, and especially abolitionists of the North, resist, and expose the absurdity" of slavery's alleged legality, and the institution, "denied thereafter all countenance and nourishment from the Constitution, will quickly perish."[15]

Of course, not every abolitionist was persuaded by such arguments. "'The Gerrit Smith Theory' of the Anti-Slavery character of the U.S. Constitution," sneered William Lloyd Garrison, "is utterly absurd and preposterous."[16]

But Smith was nothing if not persistent, and he made it part of his mission to persuade skeptical Garrisonians to see things his way. "Were you a reader of the newspapers of the Liberty Party," Smith wrote to one of Garrison's followers, in a typical 1846 letter, "you would not feel yourself authorized to take it for granted, that to hold an office under the Constitution is to be guilty of swearing to uphold slavery. On the contrary," Smith argued, "an oath to abide by the Constitution is an oath to labor for the overthrow of slavery."[17] In that same letter, Smith offered a heartfelt justification for his own heterodox position. "You ask me to join you in abandoning the Constitution. My whole heart—my whole sense of duty to God and man—forbids my doing so," he wrote. "The Constitution has put weapons into the hands of the American people entirely sufficient for slaying the monster" of slavery. Given the choice, how could any self-professed abolitionist fail to wield such weapons? "To give up the Constitution is to give up the slave."[18]

"The True Test"

Although William Lloyd Garrison would denounce the Gerrit Smith theory of the Constitution, the most significant intellectual force behind antislavery constitutionalism was not actually Smith but, rather, was the legal theorist and polemicist Lysander Spooner. Although little known today outside scholarly circles, Spooner was a key figure in the abolitionist movement and one of the more inno-vative legal and political thinkers of the nineteenth century.

Spooner was born in 1808 in Athol, Massachusetts. At the age of twenty-seven he set up shop as a lawyer in Worcester. His first professional act was to openly violate the laws of the state. At that time, Massachusetts required all would-be lawyers who lacked a college degree to first complete a five-year apprenticeship (formal law schools were not yet common in the United States). Spooner had completed neither college nor apprenticeship. He just started practicing law. At the same time, he took to the pages of the *Worcester Republican* to denounce the very law that he was then breaking. Not only did the state's apprenticeship requirement discriminate against the poor (who could not always afford college), Spooner argued, but it helped the legal establishment "keep up prices, and shut out competitors."[19] The state legislature ultimately agreed and changed the law in 1836.

Spooner's next clash with the powers that be came in the form of a confrontation with the U.S. Postal Service, which enjoyed then—as it still does now—a government-enforced monopoly over the deliv-ery of first-class mail. To demonstrate the superiority of his own free-market ideas, Spooner founded the American Letter Mail Company in 1844 and began illegally competing with the Postal Service on select routes. Once again, Spooner published a spirited legal defense of his actions. And while he enjoyed a brief victory as an entrepre-neur by providing a cheaper, more reliable service than the govern-ment did, the ensuing legal battle forced him out of business.

By then, like many Americans, Spooner was increasingly focused on the impending national crisis over slavery. With the financial backing of Gerrit Smith, Spooner joined the battle in 1845 with *The Unconstitutionality of Slavery*, a sweeping attack on the legality of the peculiar institution.

For Spooner, the protection of natural rights—the doctrine that individual liberty is inherent to human nature—was essential for constitutional legitimacy. "In order that the contract of government may be valid and lawful," Spooner insisted, it "cannot lawfully autho-rize government to destroy or take from men their natural rights; for natural rights are inalienable, and can no more be surrendered to government—which is but an association of individuals—than to a single individual."[20] Thus, any constitution that purported to sanction slavery, arguably the worst violation of natural rights short of murder, was invalid and should not be obeyed. Even "if the majority, however large, of the people of a country," all agreed to follow a proslavery constitution, "this compact of government is unlawful and void."[21]

For the sake of argument, Spooner then set aside this natural-rights-based argument. Assume that the institution of slavery can be legally permitted, Spooner wrote. Because slavery violates every tenet of natural law, that means that it can only be justified by positive, or man-made, legal strictures. And what must those strictures look like if they are to be in full accordance with existing Anglo-American legal rules? First and foremost, Spooner observed, they must be "express, explicit, distinct, unequivocal," leaving no doubt whatsoever about their proslavery status.[22] After all, the stated purpose of the U.S. Constitution is to "secure the Blessings of Liberty." If the document were to permit slavery, it had to be absolutely clear about it.

As an authority for this approach, Spooner cited the U.S. Supreme Court's 1805 ruling in the case of *United States v. Fisher*. At issue was whether federal bankruptcy law should be interpreted to prioritize one class of creditors over another when it came to the payment of certain debts. In his majority opinion, Chief Justice John Marshall wrote the following: "Where rights are infringed, where fundamental principles are overthrown, where the general system of the law is departed from, the legislative intention must be expressed with irresistible clearness, to induce a court of justice to suppose a design to affect such objects."[23]

Spooner took this rule and ran with it. "Where words are susceptible of two meanings, one consistent, and the other inconsistent, with justice and natural right," he maintained, "that meaning, and *only that* meaning, which is consistent with right, shall be attributed to them—unless other parts of the [Constitution] overrule that interpretation."[24]

Now look at the Constitution itself. "Not even the name of the thing [slavery], alleged to be sanctioned, is given."[25] Take the infa-

mous Three-Fifths Clause, which states that for purposes of taxation and political representation, state populations shall be counted
"by adding to the whole Number of free Persons, including those
bound to Service for a Term of Years, and excluding Indians not
taxed, three fifths of all other Persons." What to make of these
"other Persons"?

The Three-Fifths Clause had certainly long been understood as
an implicit acknowledgment of slavery. James Madison's published
notes on the proceedings of the 1787 Constitutional Convention, for
example, made it clear that the subject of slavery dominated many
of the debates that summer in Philadelphia. "The great divisions of
interests," Madison wrote, "did not lie between the large and small
States; It lay between the Northern and Southern."[26] Terms such as
"other Persons" were introduced to alleviate this division. In an 1819
letter, Madison acknowledged that many delegates to the Constitutional Convention "had scruples against admitting the term 'slaves'
into the Instrument. Hence the descriptive phrase."[27]

For Spooner, however, that was simply not enough to sanction
the practice legally. The phrase "other Persons," he argued, is open
to both an innocent interpretation ("partial citizens," or resident
aliens) and a malevolent one (slaves). And per the rule of "irresistible clearness" spelled out by Chief Justice Marshall in the *Fisher*
case, when faced with the choice between a constitutional interpretation that secures rights and one that subverts them, the former must always prevail over the latter. Anything less would violate
a bedrock principle of legal interpretation and thus nullify the legitimacy of the government.

Spooner also waved away those arguments rooted in the proslavery intentions of the founding fathers. "Why," Spooner asked, "in the
case of slavery, do men merely say that the Constitution *intended* to
sanction it, instead of saying distinctly, as we do in the other cases,
that it *did* sanction it?" The answer spoke for itself: "If they were to
say unequivocally that it did sanction it, they would lay themselves
under the necessity of pointing to the words that sanction it; and
they are aware that the *words alone* of the Constitution do not come
up to that point."[28]

"This is the true test for determining whether the Constitution does, or does not, sanction slavery," Spooner concluded. "Whether a court of law, strangers to the prior existence of slavery, or not assuming its prior existence to be legal—could, consistently with legal rules, judicially determine that it sanctioned slavery. Every lawyer, who deserves that name, knows that the claim for slavery could stand no such test."[29]

The Unconstitutionality of Slavery sparked a firestorm of debate among abolitionists. In Liberty Party circles, the book basically became required reading. "*Whereas*, Lysander Spooner, of Massachusetts, that man of honest heart and acute and profound intellect, has published a perfectly conclusive legal argument against the constitutionality of slavery," declared a resolution of the New York Liberty Party, adopted unanimously in 1849, "we warmly recommend to the friends of freedom, in this and other States, to supply, within the coming six months, each lawyer in their respective counties with a copy of said argument."[30]

The Garrisonians took a dimmer view. In fact, Wendell Phillips, who was effectively Garrison's second-in-command, went so far as to publish a book-length attack on Spooner's position. Spooner "bases his conclusions on a forced interpretation of legal maxims," Phillips maintained, while "the rest of his reasoning, where not logically absurd and self-contradictory, is subversive of all sound principles of Government and public faith." And that was not the worst of it. Spooner's theory was so preposterous, Phillips insisted, that it threatened to embarrass every abolitionist by association while at the same time doing lasting damage to the cause. "Any movement or party . . . founded on [Spooner's] plan, would, so soon as it grew considerable enough to attract public attention, be met by the contempt and disapprobation of every enlightened and honest man," Phillips wrote. "To trust our cause with such a leader is to ensure its shipwreck."[31]

"The Original Intent and Meaning"

Frederick Douglass followed the Spooner-Phillips debate with great interest. Writing in response to a January 23, 1847, letter from the abolitionist C. H. Chase, for example, Douglass revealed the extent to which he was then pondering Spooner's thesis. "On a close examination of the Constitution," Douglass wrote, "I am satisfied that if strictly 'construed according to its reading,' it is not a pro-slavery instrument." In other words, by 1847, Douglass had already come to accept the idea that the text of the Constitution, *by itself*, contained no direct support for slavery. But "I hold now, as I ever have done," he added, "that the original intent and meaning of the Constitution (the one given to it by the men who framed it, those who adopted it, and the one given to it by the Supreme Court of the United States) makes it a pro-slavery instrument—such an one as I cannot bring myself to vote under, or swear to support."[32]

Douglass made reference to Spooner's strict textualist argument again on February 9, 1847, except this time he used it as a weapon against one of slavery's most famous supporters. On February 2 Senator John C. Calhoun of South Carolina had released a document titled "The Address of the Southern Delegates in Congress, to Their Constituents." In it, Calhoun (joined by many congressional cosigners) blasted those Northern states and cities that were then passing what were known as "personal liberty laws," which were enacted to hinder or even block the capture and return of fugitive slaves who had escaped to free soil. Calhoun denounced such obstructionist measures as blatantly illegal under the constitutional provision governing the return of persons "held to Service or Labour." "We do not deem it necessary to undertake to refute the sophistry and subterfuges by which so plain a provision of the Constitution has been evaded, and in effect, annulled," he wrote. As far as Calhoun was concerned, "it is impossible for any [constitutional] provision to be more free from ambiguity or doubt."[33]

Not so fast, Douglass shot back in a *North Star* editorial. "We deem it unfortunate for these honorable manstealers, that in no instance have they been able to find a word in [the Constitution] which bears the definition of slaves or slavery." To be sure, Douglass granted, the Constitution was "*intended* to bolster slavery," yet the language "has been so ambiguously worded as to bear a very different construction; and taken with the preamble of that instrument," which says that the Constitution's purpose is to "secure the Blessings of Liberty," the document may undoubtedly be read to give "the very opposite of the construction given it by this wily band of slaveholders."[34]

Indeed, Douglass continued, the text of the Constitution, by itself, contains nothing that is actively friendly toward slavery. "Blot slavery from existence, and the whole framework of the Constitution might remain unchanged," he maintained. Douglass then went further, adopting Spooner's argument that the "true test" was "whether a court of law, strangers to the prior existence of slavery . . . could, consistently with legal rules, judicially determine that [the Constitution] sanctioned slavery." Here is how Douglass put it in his own words: "Suppose a man from another country should read that clause of the American Constitution, with no other knowledge of the character of American institutions than what he derived from the reading of that instrument. . . . Would any one pretend that the clause in question would be thought to apply to slaves? We think not."[35] Douglass had not yet accepted Spooner's entire theory, but he was happily making use of the intellectual ammunition that Spooner provided.

Gerrit Smith read that *North Star* editorial on the day that it was published and immediately fired off an approving letter to its author. "Your comments on Calhoun's manifesto," Smith wrote to Douglass, "cheer me with the hope that you are on the very eve of wielding the Federal Constitution for the abolition of American slavery." The time had come, he urged Douglass, to go all the way. "With you and your paper on the right side, something more can be done for Liberty than has been done."[36]

But Douglass was nowhere near that point yet, as he made clear in a public response to Smith's letter that appeared a few weeks later. "The Constitution of the United States, standing alone, and construed only in the light of its letter, without reference to the opinions of the men who framed and adopted it, or to the uniform, universal and undeviating practice of the nation under it, from the time of its adoption until now, is not a pro-slavery instrument," Douglass conceded in the *North Star*. "Of this admission we are perfectly willing to give our esteemed friend Gerrit Smith, and all who think with him on this subject, the fullest benefit."[37] But Douglass also gave the full-

est benefit to the intentions of the document's framers. "Slaveholders took a large share in making" the Constitution, he observed. "It
was made in view of the existence of slavery, and in a manner well
calculated to aid and strengthen that heaven-daring crime."[38] At this
point, Douglass was still a practicing Garrisonian.

Douglass took aim at Smith's reasoning again two weeks later,
writing in the March 30, 1849, issue of the *North Star* that until Smith
provided "some fixed and settled legal rules sustaining his views,"
Douglass would continue to interpret the Constitution "not only
in the light of its letter, but in view of its history [and] the meaning
attached to it by its framers." Douglass did, however, make one small
but noteworthy concession in Smith's direction. "We have not read
law very extensively," Douglass admitted, "but so far as we have read,
we have found many rules of interpretation favoring [the Garrisonian]
mode of understanding the Constitution of the United States, and
none against it, though there may be such."[39] Put differently, Douglass
was still weighing the evidence, and he was still open to persuasion.

A little over a year later, on April 5, 1850, Douglass took his biggest
step yet away from Garrison and toward the Spooner-Smith position. Commenting on a speech by the antislavery New York senator
William H. Seward, who would soon help to found the Republican
Party and later serve as secretary of state under President Abraham
Lincoln, Douglass described the Constitution in a new, more abolitionist friendly way. "Liberty and Slavery," he wrote, "are both" in
the document. That new description carried significant implications.
After all, under this view, when slaveholders swore an oath to support
the Constitution, they were swearing an oath to support a government compact that was at least partially hostile to slavery. "If [they]
adopt the preamble, with Liberty and Justice," Douglass declared,
"[they] must repudiate the enacting clauses, with Kidnapping and
Slaveholding."[40] In his heart of hearts, Douglass wrote, "every slaveholder knows" that if he swears to uphold the Constitution, "his
whole life gives an emphatic lie to his solemn vow."[41] It was Douglass's most direct constitutional argument to date against slavery.

Nine months later, Douglass took an even more fateful step. On
January 21, 1851, he informed Gerrit Smith that while he still did not

fully subscribe to Smith's position, "I am so much impressed by your reasoning that I have decided to let Slaveholders and their Northern abettors have the Laboring *oar* in putting a proslavery interpretation upon the Constitution." In other words, Douglass would no longer take Garrison's side in public debates over this grave and fundamental matter. "I am sick and tired of arguing on the slaveholders' side of this question," Douglass wrote, "although they are doubtless right so far as the intentions of the framers of the Constitution are concerned."[42] That was January. By May the transformation was complete.

"A Radical Change in My Opinions"

Frederick Douglass and Gerrit Smith exchanged a great many letters throughout the course of their long partnership in the fight against slavery. But it is safe to say that Douglass's letter to Smith on May 1, 1851, carried a special weight for both parties. "I am prepared to treat slavery as a system of *'lawless violence'* incapable of being legalized," Douglass informed Smith. "I am prepared for those rules of interpretation which when applied to the Constitution make its details harmonize with its declared objects in its preamble. I am satisfied on those points, and my heart is strong."[43] After years of debate and discussion, those words must have come as music to Smith's ears.

In his 1855 book, *My Bondage and My Freedom*, the second of the three autobiographies that he would write, Douglass reflected on the long, laborious process by which he came to change his mind about the relationship between slavery and the Constitution. It required nothing less than "a reconsideration of the whole subject," he wrote. He studied, "with some care, not only the just and proper rules of legal interpretation, but the origin, design, nature, rights, powers, and duties of civil government, and also the relations which human beings sustain to it."[44] The influence of Lysander Spooner is evident in nearly every word of that explanation. *The Unconstitutionality of Slavery* had clearly left its mark on Douglass's mind.

Douglass's close study of constitutional history also helped to alter his point of view. "In reading the sentiments of the most influential men of the period, and to which the Constitution was framed and adopted," Douglass explained in an 1851 editorial, "it is evident that slavery was looked upon as a great evil—not merely regarded with aversion by the North, but by many of the most distinguished men at the South." In other words, perhaps the case for the proslavery intentions of the founding fathers had been vastly overstated. For example, Douglass pointed out, "the writings of Washington, Franklin, Jefferson, Adams, Madison, Monroe, Hamilton, Luther Martin, Patrick Henry, John Jay, and a host of other great men, fathers of the Republic," all contained a variety of antislavery sentiments. "Whoever else might have intended that the Constitution should protect slavery," Douglass concluded, "there were those among the most illustrious in the country who entertained no such intention."[45]

Douglass broke the news about his change of mind to the Garrisonians at the annual meeting of the American Anti-Slavery Society in Syracuse, New York, on May 9, 1851. The *North Star*, Douglass told the gathering, would henceforth speak out against slavery on constitutional grounds. "Here was a radical change in my opinions," Douglass acknowledged. Naturally, he expected that his announcement would cause controversy. But he was simply unprepared for the extreme vilifications that followed. "The common punishment of apostates," Douglass later observed, "was mine."[46]

That was putting it mildly. Not only did the Garrisonians attack Douglass as wrongheaded, but they denounced him as an unprincipled sellout. "There is roguery somewhere!" Garrison declared, implying that Douglass had only switched his views in exchange for Gerrit Smith's money.[47] It was a cheap smear—but it stuck. The Garrisonians would unfairly caricature Douglass as Smith's puppet on plenty more occasions in the years to come.

Adding further insult to injury, Garrison also began including excerpts from Douglass's writings in a section of the *Liberator* known as the Refuge of Oppression. This column, which was featured prominently on the front page of every issue, featured excerpts and quotations from proslavery newspapers and periodicals, all carefully selected so that abolitionists might know the minds of their enemies. "Why," one correspondent asked Garrison in 1853, "do you place [Douglass's] articles in the 'Refuge of Oppression,' side by side with the vilest pro-slavery venom from the vilest sheets in the land?" Garrison replied that Douglass "has lost much of moral power, and will finally lose what yet remains."[48]

Of course, Garrison's negative reaction was not universally shared among abolitionists. In 1852, for example, Harriet Beecher Stowe, author of the bestselling book *Uncle Tom's Cabin*, wrote Garrison a letter expressing her disapproval of the manner in which Douglass had been treated in the pages of the *Liberator*. Having just interviewed Douglass herself, Stowe wrote that her "impression was far more satisfactory than [she] had anticipated" in light of what Garrison had been writing and saying. "I am satisfied that his change of sentiments was not a mere political one but a genuine growth of his own conviction," she wrote. "You speak of him as an apostate," Stowe concluded. "I cannot but regard this language as unjustly severe. . . . Where is this work of excommunication to end—Is there but one true anti-slavery church and all others infidels?—Who shall declare which it is?"[49]

As far as political divorces go, the Garrison-Douglass split was an ugly one. For a time, the two had labored practically side by side; they had traveled together, shared the same humble lodgings, trod the same stages, faced down the same jeering mobs. But they had also been growing apart philosophically, and the bitter debate over the meaning of the Constitution proved to be the breaking point. It also brought out the worst in Garrison. Indeed, Garrison could still be found besmirching Douglass in 1860, as the nation around them was tottering on the brink of civil war. Douglass is "thoroughly base and selfish," Garrison complained in a letter that year. "In fact, he reveals himself more and more to me as destitute of every principle of honor, ungrateful to the last degree, and malevolent in spirit. He is not worthy of respect, confidence, or countenance."[50]

Douglass was both hurt and infuriated by such attacks from his once-revered mentor—but he refused to be deterred from his new course. The Constitution "is our warrant for the abolition of slavery in every state in the American union," he declared.[51] Equipped with that belief, Douglass would enter the political arena and redouble his efforts against the slave system.

"Free Soil, Free Speech, Free Labor, and Free Men"

At the same time that Frederick Douglass was rising in the Garrisonian ranks, an upstart third-party political movement was building steam among antislavery activists. One of the key figures in that movement was a tenacious Ohio lawyer named Salmon P. Chase. "There was a dignity and grandeur about [Chase] which marked him as one born great," Douglass would later write. Chase "had known me in early anti-slavery days and had welcomed me to his home and his table when to do so was a strange thing . . . and the fact was by no means an insignificant one."[52] In the years to come, Chase's career would intersect with Douglass's in a number of important ways.

Chase was born in Cornish, New Hampshire, in 1808. In 1830 he set out for Cincinnati, Ohio, then a fast-growing commercial center, where he set up shop as a lawyer. Much like what happened with Gerrit Smith, Chase was radicalized into antislavery politics after experiencing antiabolitionist violence at close range. That violence centered on the journalist James G. Birney, who edited an abolitionist newspaper in Cincinnati called the *Philanthropist*. The Kentucky-born Birney was a former slaveowner who had freed his slaves and joined the fight against the peculiar institution. The existence of his paper ruffled more than a few proslavery feathers in that part of Ohio, which shared a border with slaveholding Kentucky. Events came to a head in the summer of 1836. On July 12 a proslavery mob broke into the building and destroyed the printing press that Birney used. The vandals also destroyed an entire print run of the *Philanthropist*, which was just about to be released. Two weeks later, the mob went hunting for Birney himself.

"I heard with disgust and horror the mob violence directed against the Anti-Slavery Press and Anti-Slavery men of Cincinnati in 1836," Chase later recalled. "I was opposed at this time to the views of the abolitionists, but I now recognized the slave power as the great enemy of freedom of speech [and] freedom of the press and freedom of the person. I took an open part against the mob." When he learned that the mob was out searching for Birney, Chase went to the house where the editor was rumored to be hiding. "I stood in the doorway, and told them calmly but resolutely, no one could pass." Chase himself was then threatened. "One, who seemed a ring-leader, said I should answer for this. I told him I could be found at any time." The mob finally dispersed after the mayor appeared and told the crowd that Birney was not holed up inside. "From this time on," Chase observed, "I became a decided opponent of Slavery and the Slave Power."[53]

From the outset, Chase's training in the law shaped his work as an antislavery activist. "I differed from Mr. Garrison and others as to the means by which the Slave Power could be best overthrown and Slavery most safely and fitly abolished under our American Constitution," he would say. Where he did not differ from the Garrisonians was "in the conviction that these objects were of paramount importance."[54]

One big difference between Chase and Garrison was Chase's embrace of electoral politics. In fact, by the early 1840s, Chase had already established himself as a leader of the Ohio Liberty Party. At the 1841 state convention, for example, Chase played a central role in drafting the party's official resolutions. "His hand," observed biographer John Niven, "was quite obvious in the resolutions that called for free labor as opposed to slave labor, and stated the federal Constitution to be an antislavery document."[55] In a letter written that same year, Chase told a correspondent that he was "fully persuaded that no mode [would] be so effectual in bringing the whole question of slavery before the people as Antislavery political action." As Chase saw it, slavery was "a power antagonistic to free labor," it was "an influence perverting our Government from its true scope and end," and it was "an institution strictly local, but now escaped from its proper limits and threatening to overshadow and nullify whatever is most valuable in our political system."[56]

The idea of slavery as a "strictly local" institution that had escaped its "proper limits" was not original to Chase, though it would become a centerpiece of his constitutional thought. The idea had already been discussed by the abolitionist Theodore Dwight Weld in his 1836 essay "The Power of Congress over Slavery in the District of Columbia." According to Weld, Congress may only exercise those powers granted to it by the Constitution. And like it or not, Congress possessed no general power to overturn state laws, which meant that Congress could not touch slavery in those states in which it already existed. To be clear, Weld wrote, "the Constitution no where recognizes the right to 'slave property,' *but merely the fact that the states have jurisdiction each in its own limits, and that there are certain 'persons' within their jurisdictions 'held to service' by their own laws.*"[57]

At the same time, Weld continued, the Constitution *did* grant the federal government multiple powers to abolish or constrain slavery on federal land and in those areas that were under the control of the federal government. Among such powers was the authority to abolish the foreign slave trade beginning in 1808, which Congress had promptly exercised that very year. There was also the power, spelled out in Article I, "to regulate Commerce . . . among the several States." Put differently, Congress had the authority to regulate the lucrative interstate slave trade out of existence. And then, of course, there was the congressional power to "exercise exclusive Legislation in all Cases whatsoever, over . . . the Seat of the Government of the United States." In short, Congress had every right to abolish slavery in the District of Columbia. In time, this argument would become known by the motto Freedom National, Slavery Sectional, and it would become a rallying cry for both the Free-Soil Party, which was founded in 1848, and the Republican Party, which was founded in 1854.

Chase further expanded on the "freedom national" argument by adding his own skilled legal analysis to it. For example, Chase used it as a legal weapon for fighting the Fugitive Slave Act all the way up to the U.S. Supreme Court. In the 1847 case of *Jones v. Van Zandt*, Chase argued that an Ohio farmer who assisted several runaway slaves should not be seen as a criminal in the eyes of the Constitution— nor should the runaways. "It was the clear understanding of all parties concerned in the establishment of the National Government," Chase maintained, "that the practice of slaveholding was inconsistent with the principles on which that government was founded." To be sure, slavery "might be tolerated or legalized in certain states, with whose legislation the General Government could not interfere," but "it should receive no national sanction whatever."[58]

In other words, according to Chase, not only was the Fugitive Slave Act unenforceable by the federal government, but Congress had the rightful power to immediately abolish slavery in the District of Columbia and to outlaw the practice in all federal territories, thereby preventing new slave states from forming and entering the union. In time, as the free states came to definitively outnumber the slave states, the peculiar institution's grip on the commanding heights of government power could be broken forever.

In an 1856 letter to the abolitionist Theodore Parker, Chase explained how he expected such views to play out in practice. "The General Government has power to prohibit slavery everywhere outside of Slave States. A great majority of the people now accept this," he wrote. So, "I say, then, take the conceded proposition and make it practical. Make it a living reality! Then you have taken a great first step. Slavery is *denationalized*." From there, he continued, "encouraged by national example, by the sympathies, cheering words and liberal aid of good men and patriots," antislavery sentiment would grow inside the slave states. "By-and-by, and not far off," Chase declared, "you will come to the . . . idea, 'no slavery in America!'"[59]

It was a powerful vision of antislavery constitutionalism. To be sure, it was a somewhat less radical vision than the one favored by Alvan Stewart, Lysander Spooner, Gerrit Smith, and (eventually) Frederick Douglass, who maintained that the Constitution empowered the federal government to outlaw slavery *everywhere*, including even in those states in which it already existed. Still, Chase's view was more than radical enough in the eyes of the slaveholders, who immediately understood that it posed a mortal threat to the stability, growth, and long-term survival of slavery. Chase was seen as doubly threatening, because his vision was rooted in such venerable principles of American law. Douglass, of course, later rooted his radical vision in those same venerable principles.

The Supreme Court, which was then led by Chief Justice Roger Taney, the future author of the *Dred Scott* decision, rejected Chase's arguments in the *Van Zandt* case. "The constitution itself," the court insisted, "flung its shield, for security, over such property as is in controversy in the present case, and the right to pursue and reclaim it within the limits of another State."[60]

Undeterred, Chase soldiered on. Congress "has no power to legislate on the subject of slavery in the States," he would acknowledge. But it does have the power "to prevent [slavery's] extension, and to prohibit its existence within the sphere of the exclusive jurisdiction of the General Government."[61] In 1848 Chase succeeded in writing those views into the national platform of the new Free-Soil Party, a party, incidentally, which he had just helped to found. "No more Slave States and no more Slave Territory," the Chase-penned platform declared. "Let the soil of our extensive domains be kept free, for the hardy pioneers of our own land, and the oppressed and banished of other lands seeking homes of comfort and fields of enterprise in the New World."[62] Chase also coined the new party's motto: Free Soil, Free Speech, Free Labor, and Free Men.[63]

Chase had a massive influence on the course of antislavery politics in the two decades before the Civil War. In the words of historian Eric Foner, "Chase's interpretation of the Constitution . . . formed the legal basis for the political program which was created by the Liberty party and inherited in large part by the Free Soilers and Republicans."[64] But Chase was more than just a thinker. He also spread his ideas as an energetic political organizer, working first for the Liberty Party, then for the Free-Soilers, and finally for the Republicans, whose national platforms in both 1856 and 1860 made explicit constitutional arguments against the spread of slavery—arguments that had been honed to a cutting edge over the years by Chase himself.

Chase was also an accomplished politician in his own right. In 1849 he was elected to the U.S. Senate as a Free-Soil candidate. From that lofty position, he loudly opposed the addition of new slave states to the union. In 1855, running as a Free-Soil Democrat, he was elected as governor of Ohio. In 1857 he was reelected to that job as a Republican. In 1860 he ran for the presidency, only to lose the Republican nomination to Abraham Lincoln. Then, during the opening years of the Civil War, Chase served as the secretary of the treasury for the Lincoln administration. Finally, in 1864, Lincoln brought Chase full circle, appointing him to the U.S. Supreme Court, where Chase would replace Roger Taney, whose court had ruled against him in the *Van Zandt* case, as chief justice of the United States.

"Power to Prevent the Increase of Slavery"

Salmon P. Chase had a point when it came to slavery and the federal government. In terms of both its text and its history, the Constitution did contain several provisions that made freedom, rather than slavery, the watchword of the national authorities. Consider Article I, Section 9, which said that Congress could prohibit the "importation of such Persons as any of the States now existing shall think proper to admit," starting in 1808. Put differently, the Constitution granted the federal government the full authority to completely outlaw the foreign slave trade. This was no small thing. Indeed, it was a massive grant of federal power that came at the expense of the slaveholders and of the slaveholding states. What is more, the power to outlaw the foreign slave trade almost did not make it into the final version of the document. The story of how it did make it into the Constitution reveals the presence of antislavery sentiments among a number of the framers.

The story goes like this. On August 6, 1787, the first draft of the Constitution was circulated among the delegates at the Constitutional Convention in Philadelphia. According to Article VII, Section 4, of that draft, "No tax or duty shall be laid by the Legislature ... on the migration or importation of such persons as the several States shall think proper to admit; nor shall such migration or importation be prohibited."[65] Put differently, Congress was initially *forbidden* from abolishing the foreign slave trade. The slaveholders were to enjoy constitutional protection on this issue forever.

But that prohibition on federal interference with the foreign slave trade did not sit well with every delegate. When the provision finally came up for discussion, Luther Martin of Maryland proposed that it be totally rewritten "so as to allow a prohibition ... on the importation of slaves." In Martin's view, "slaves weakened one part of the Union which the other parts were bound to protect: the privilege of importing them was therefore unreasonable." Furthermore, "it was inconsistent with the principles of the revolution and dishonorable to the American character to have such a feature in the Constitution."[66]

Those objections kicked off two days of sharp debate. According to John Rutledge of South Carolina, the whole matter boiled down to "whether the Southern States shall or shall not be parties to the Union." He urged "the Northern States [to] consult their interest" and leave the proslavery provision alone.[67] Oliver Ellsworth of Connecticut was prepared to do exactly that. "Let every State import what it pleases," he argued. "The morality or wisdom of slavery are considerations belonging to the States themselves."[68]

Charles Pinckney of South Carolina took the proslavery position even further. "South Carolina can never receive the plan if it prohibits the slave trade," he threatened.[69] The other delegates certainly paid attention to that. Roger Sherman of Connecticut, for instance, piped up to say that while he did not personally approve of the slave trade, "yet as the States were now possessed of the right to import slaves" and "as it was expedient to have as few objections as possible to the proposed scheme of government," he "thought it best to leave the matter as we find it."[70]

George Mason of Virginia, who was himself a slaveowner, disagreed entirely with Pinckney and Sherman. "This infernal traffic originated in the avarice of British merchants," Mason said. The new Constitution should therefore have nothing to do with it. "As to the States being in possession of the Right to import," Mason continued, "this was the case with many other rights, now to be properly given up." In his view, it was "essential in every point of view that the General Government should have power to prevent the increase of slavery."[71]

In the end, after much haggling, the offending provision was deleted, and the document took on the familiar form that we recognize today. To be clear, the representatives of the free states did strike a bargain with their slaveholding counterparts; they made a compromise with slavery. But as Chase (and others) never tired of pointing out, that compromise also included the fact that the Constitution granted the federal government significant powers to restrict slavery's spread and thus imperil its future existence.

"My Motto Is Extermination"

Frederick Douglass would never become the sort of consummate political insider that Salmon P. Chase—the future senator, governor, presidential cabinet member, and Supreme Court justice—would prove to be. For starters, Douglass never held elected office. Nor did he ever attempt the tricky job of organizing and maintaining a winning political coalition. Instead, Douglass would have his greatest impact on American politics as a kind of perennial outsider. To be sure, he often made common cause with antislavery politicians and parties—Liberty, Free-Soil, and Republican—and he eagerly took part in the great political debates of the day, including presidential contests. But his voice remained that of a radical. He was sometimes supportive and sometimes cajoling, but always he was seeking to push the system in a more thoroughgoing abolitionist direction. In a sense, Douglass served as the conscience of the antislavery political movement. And his influence in that role proved to be far-reaching.

For example, consider Douglass's dealings with the Free-Soilers. In the eyes of some of his more radical allies, this new party was not worth the trouble. "I have never adopted its absurd and contradictory motto, *'freedom national, slavery sectional,'*" Lysander Spooner would say, adding that he had "no sympathy" for the Free-Soil Party's "pusillanimous and criminal sentiment. . . . I do not believe the Constitution authorizes any such compromises [and] I hope . . . to see freedom and slavery meet face to face, with no question between them except which shall conquer and which shall die."[72]

Douglass agreed with Spooner on the constitutional question, as well as on the ultimate fate of slavery, but he differed when it came to the matter of advancing abolitionist principles. In fact, Douglass had warmed to the idea of antislavery political activism even before he warmed to the idea of an antislavery Constitution. "We must go on and lead the Free Soilers," Douglass had told the Rhode Island Anti-Slavery Society in 1848.[73] That same year, Douglass's paper, the *North Star*, voiced its support for the Free-Soil presidential candidacy of Martin Van Buren. Four years later, in July 1852, Douglass could be found plotting with Gerrit Smith in preparation for

the National Free-Soil Convention that would be held the following month in Pittsburgh, Pennsylvania. "Mere *free soil*, I am sure,
will not satisfy the masses who will attend the Convention," Douglass wrote to Smith. "The abolitionists of the west are in advance
of their leaders. They are ready for a more certain sound than that
which has of late called them out to battle. Can you not go and give
them that sound?"[74]

In the end, Douglass and Smith both attended the convention, but
it was Douglass who brought the noise. He was recognized shortly
after arriving and was promptly nominated to serve as one of the
convention's officers. He was then elected to that official role by wide
acclamation. Shortly after that, he was called upon to speak. Douglass had not actually planned to give a speech that day, but his long
experience on the lecture circuit did not let him down. He simply
got up and spoke without notes.

"I have come here, not so much a free soiler as others have come,"
he admitted to the crowd of two thousand. "I am, of course, for cir-
cumscribing and damaging slavery in every way I can. But my motto
is extermination—not only in New Mexico, but in New Orleans—
not only in California but in South Carolina." Slavery, he declared,
"has no rightful existence anywhere."[75] Here was Douglass, right in
the heart of the growing campaign for Freedom National, Slavery
Sectional, and he was preaching the hard-line abolitionist constitutionalism of Spooner and Smith. And a significant portion of the
audience was loudly cheering along.

Douglass also took the opportunity that day to urge the Free-
Soilers to distinguish themselves from the sorry state of the two major
political parties. Both the Whigs and the Democrats, he observed,
in their recent national conventions, "acted in open contempt of the
antislavery sentiment of the North, by incorporating, as the corner-
stone of their two platforms, the infamous" Fugitive Slave Law of
1850. That law had stripped suspected runaways of virtually all legal
protections, even in those states that had passed "personal liberty
laws." The Free-Soil Party, Douglass argued, must oppose this legislative outrage. "In making your Platform," he maintained, "nothing is to be gained by a timid policy."[76]

To be sure, he continued, "it has been said that our fathers entered into a covenant for this slave catching." He was referring to the notion that the founding fathers wrote their proslavery intentions into the Constitution. But "if you look over the list of your rights, you do not find among them any right to make a slave of your brother. . . . I hope, therefore, that you will take the ground that this slavery is a system, not only of wrong, but is of a lawless character, and can neither be Christianized nor legalized."[77] Then, after waiting for the applause to die down, Douglass made a final plea for the convention to take a stand on behalf of abolitionist principles, rather than political expediency. "It has been said that we ought to take the position to gain the greatest number of voters, but that is wrong," Douglass declared. "The man who is right is a majority. . . . If he does not represent what we are, he represents what we ought to be."[78]

The Free-Soilers did not disappoint. Although the party's 1852 platform did continue to maintain that "slavery is sectional, and freedom national," it also contained a number of strident antislavery stances that undoubtedly warmed Douglass's heart. "Slavery is a sin against God and a crime against man, which no human enactment nor usage can make right," the platform declared. The Fugitive Slave Act of 1850, it said, "is repugnant to the Constitution, to the principles of the common law, to the spirit of Christianity, and to the sentiments of the civilized world. We therefore deny its binding force upon the American people." As for "the persevering and importune demands of the slave power for more slave States, new slave Territories, and the nationalization of slavery, our distinct and final answer," the platform declared, "is—no more slave States, no slave Territory, no nationalized slavery, and no national legislation for the extradition of slaves."[79]

It was not the fully radical vision that Frederick Douglass favored, of course. But it was still a bold piece of antislavery constitutionalism, and Douglass could work with it. "We attended the Convention in Pittsburgh with very little hope that it would present to the country a platform sufficiently anti-slavery for us to stand upon," Douglass told the readers of his paper. Thankfully, he had found himself pleasantly surprised. The Free-Soil platform "will, doubtless, meet with enthusiastic support, even among the radical members of 'the Liberty Party.'" To be clear, Douglass acknowledged, "it does not certainly say all we should like to have said, but it is a long step in the right direction."[80] In a few years' time, Douglass would make a nearly identical point about another rising force in the field of antislavery politics: Abraham Lincoln.

"Our Preferences Cannot Hesitate"

Over the course of three busy months in the spring and summer of 1858, Abraham Lincoln, the Republican challenger, and Stephen A. Douglas, the Democratic incumbent, stumped the state of Illinois in their race for the U.S. Senate. In addition to speaking separately at numerous party rallies, the two men shared the stage on seven different occasions. The verbal duels that resulted would go down in the history books as the famous Lincoln-Douglas debates.

The name *Frederick Douglass* kept coming up. In the first of their seven statewide debates, for example, this one held in Ottawa, Illinois, on August 21, Senator Douglas attacked Lincoln for "following the example and lead of all the little Abolition orators, who go around and lecture in the basements of schools and churches." Lincoln "reads from the Declaration of Independence, that all men are created equal," Douglas said, "and then asks how can you deprive a negro of that equality which God and the Declaration of Independence awards to him." This description was not intended as a compliment. "For my own part," Douglas declared, "I do not regard the negro as my equal, and positively deny that he is my brother." Lincoln, he scoffed, "is worthy of a medal . . . from Fred Douglass for his abolitionism."[81]

Senator Douglas employed a similar tactic a few weeks later at their debate in Charleston. Douglas claimed that during the 1854 statewide elections, "in the northern part of the state I found Lincoln's ally, in the person of Fred. Douglass, THE NEGRO, preaching Abolition doctrines, while Lincoln was discussing the same principles down here."[82] Douglas then told the Charleston audience that he had in his possession a recent "speech made by Fred. Douglass . . . in which he conjures all the friends of negro equality and negro citizenship to rally as one man around Abraham Lincoln, the perfect embodiment of their principles, and by all means defeat Stephen A. Douglas."[83]

Abraham Lincoln was not in fact the perfect embodiment of abolitionist principles, as virtually every abolitionist alive at the time would have attested. For one thing, Lincoln was not an abolitionist at all, a point that Lincoln himself repeatedly emphasized. Nor did Lincoln want to see the federal government make trouble for slavery in those states in which the institution already existed. Frederick Douglass, by contrast, favored the complete abolition of slavery everywhere in America.

But Stephen Douglas was not entirely wrong to see certain similarities between the Republican politician and the abolitionist agitator. Indeed, from the standpoint of the slaveholders, Lincoln and Douglass both stood for ideas that posed deadly threats to the future of the peculiar institution.

For instance, consider how Lincoln and Douglass each addressed the constitutionality of slavery in speeches that they delivered, less than a month apart from each other, in early 1860. Speaking at the Cooper Institute in New York City on February 27, Lincoln launched one of his most forceful attacks on the idea that Congress lacked the authority to interfere with slavery on federal land. That proslavery position rests on "an assumed constitutional right of [slaveholders] to take slaves into the Federal Territories, and to hold them there as property," Lincoln noted. "But no such right is specifically written in the Constitution." The document "is literally silent about any such right."[84]

Indeed, Lincoln continued, "neither the word 'slave' nor the word 'slavery' is to be found in the Constitution." Even those provisions considered to be proslavery, such as the Three-Fifths Clause, used the term *person* while carefully avoiding the term *slave*. And why was this done? "To exclude from the Constitution the idea that there could be property in man."[85]

As for the intentions of the founding fathers, Lincoln continued, none other than George Washington, the first president of the United States and a member of the 1787 Constitutional Convention in Philadelphia, signed into law a bill, passed by the first Congress, that enforced the Northwest Ordinance of 1787, which banned slavery in federal territory. "As those fathers marked it," Lincoln declared, "so let [slavery] be again marked, as an evil not to be extended."[86]

Speaking in Glasgow, Scotland, on March 26, Frederick Douglass also stressed, as he had been doing since the late 1840s, the Constitution's lack of textual support for slavery. "The intentions of those who framed the Constitution, be they good or bad, for slavery or against slavery, are to be respected so far, and so far only, as we find those intentions plainly stated in the Constitution."[87] So, what do we find in the Constitution? "No such words as 'African slave trade'" and "no such words as 'slave insurrections' are anywhere used in that instrument."[88]

But suppose those words did appear in the text, Douglass continued. What of it? The provision governing the "importation" of certain persons, "if made to refer to the African slave trade at all, makes the Constitution anti-slavery rather than for slavery." That is because it handed the federal government the awesome power to abolish the foreign slave trade. "It looked to the abolition of slavery rather than to its perpetuity."[89]

By the same token, take a closer look at the federal powers to "suppress Insurrections" and protect each state "against domestic Violence." According to both the slaveholders and the Garrisonians, Douglass observed, those two clauses committed the federal government to the job of forcibly keeping the slaves in chains. But do the clauses really do that? "If it should turn out that slavery is a source of insurrection," Douglass reasoned, "that there is no security from insurrection while slavery lasts, why, the Constitution would be best obeyed by putting an end to slavery, and an anti-slavery Congress would do that very thing." So much for the "so-called slave-holding provisions of the American Constitution."[90]

These two speeches also revealed another important similarity between Lincoln and Douglass: not only did they both argue that the federal government was empowered to prevent the spread of slavery on federal land, but they both maintained that the federal government should not hesitate in doing so. "Can we, while our votes will prevent it," Lincoln asked the audience at the Cooper Institute, "allow [slavery] to spread into the National Territories, and to over-throw us here in these free states? If our sense of duty forbids this, then let us stand by our duty fearlessly and effectively."[91]

Douglass struck a similar note of resolve in Glasgow. "If 35,000 slaveholders, by devoting their energies to that single end," have bent the Constitution in favor of slavery, "now let the freemen of the North, who have the power in their own hands, and who can make the American Government just what they think fit, resolve to blot out for ever the foul and haggard crime."[92]

Two months later, Lincoln secured the Republican Party's nomination for the presidency of the United States. Douglass had closely followed the nomination fight as it played out at the Chicago convention. When it was all said and done, he admitted that he still had his doubts about both the Republican Party and its new leader. But at the same time, Douglass also knew how to spot antislavery potential when he saw it. "We are sorry that the hosts of freedom could not have been led forth upon a higher platform, and have had inscribed upon their banners, 'Death to Slavery,' instead of 'No more Slave States,'" Douglass wrote shortly after learning the news of Lincoln's nomination. But "as between the hosts of Slavery propagandism and the Republican party—incomplete as is its platform of principles—our preferences cannot hesitate." Indeed, Douglass concluded, "to turn the tide of the National Administration against the man-stealers of this country and in favor of even a partial application of the principles of justice, is a glorious achievement, and we hope for its success."[93]

"The Blessings of Liberty"

Was Frederick Douglass right? Did the Constitution empower the federal government to abolish slavery in every state in the union? Did the document empower the federal government to abolish slavery anywhere in the United States?

Douglass's argument in favor of an abolitionist Constitution began with the document's Preamble. The Constitution was written, the Preamble said, to "establish Justice, insure domestic Tranquility, provide for the common defence, promote the general Welfare, and secure the Blessings of Liberty to ourselves and our Posterity." Every con-stitutional provision that followed, Douglass maintained, must be interpreted in light of those overarching goals. Furthermore, because the Constitution never once used the words *slave* or *slavery*, it was impossible to sustain a proslavery interpretation while remaining faithful to the Preamble's liberty-minded objectives—not to men-tion remaining faithful to the Constitution's overall role as a protec-tor of individual rights.

It was a tight legal argument, and it definitely appealed to a num-ber of skilled lawyers at the time. But as we have seen, the historical evidence also shows that the Constitution was designed to offer cer-tain protections for domestic slavery, and some of the Constitution's language was understood to do precisely that by those who framed and ratified the document. Of course, as Salmon P. Chase repeat-edly pointed out, the document was also originally understood to contain a number of antislavery provisions that granted significant antislavery powers to the federal government. In that sense, Chase's constitutional argument, Freedom National, Slavery Sectional, is arguably more plausible than the all-encompassing constitutional argument favored by Douglass.

To my mind, Douglass made perhaps his most persuasive consti-tutional argument on April 5, 1850, when he was still wrestling with the competing theories of Lysander Spooner and William Lloyd Garrison. The Constitution, he wrote on that day, is "at war with itself." Look carefully and you will find "two distinct and hostile elements" in it, he said. "Liberty and Slavery—opposite as Heaven and Hell—are both in the Constitution."[94] That sounds about right when it comes to the document that was written in Philadelphia in the summer of 1787.

Whether you fully agree with Douglass or not, there is no deny-ing the overall force of his legal arguments and the significant impact they had on the broader antislavery movement. In the coming years, as the nation lurched ever closer toward secession and armed con-flict, he would make perhaps his greatest impact of all. At a time when the Constitution was "at war with itself," Frederick Douglass would help to lead the fight on the side of freedom.

3

"This Hell-Black Judgment of the Supreme Court"

I n the early months of 1836, around the same time that John Quincy Adams was fighting the gag rule in the House of Representatives, a similar battle over the silencing of abolitionist petitions was playing out in the Senate. At the heart of that conflict stood one of slavery's loudest and most uncompromising defenders. John C. Calhoun occupied the commanding heights of American politics for the better part of four decades. Born in Abbeville, South Carolina, in 1782, he served as secretary of war for President James Monroe, as secretary of state for President John Tyler, and as vice president for two very different administrations, those of John Quincy Adams and Andrew Jackson, respectively. But it was from his perch in the Senate that the South Carolinian wielded perhaps his greatest influence of all, an influence that he used time and time again on behalf of the peculiar institution.

On March 9, 1836, Senator Calhoun rose, not for the first time, to sing the praises of human bondage. Two months earlier, Senator Thomas Morris of Ohio had presented a pair of petitions sent by citizens of his state "praying for the abolition of slavery in the District of Columbia." In response, Calhoun had promptly moved that the petitions be rejected by the Senate. "Congress had no jurisdiction on the subject," he insisted, "no more in this District than the State of South Carolina."[1] That exchange initiated weeks of senatorial debate. In March, Calhoun spoke at length in defense of his position.

"Why should these petitions be received?" Calhoun demanded. Why should the Senate "receive what all acknowledge to be highly dangerous and inflammatory?"[2] Calhoun was well aware of the constitutional argument, made by John Quincy Adams and others, that a congressional rejection of abolitionist petitions amounted to a violation of the First Amendment, which secured "the right of the people . . . to petition the Government for a redress of grievances."

But Calhoun simply waved that argument away. "If it shall be shown," he maintained, "not only that we are not bound to receive" the petitions but that to receive them "would yield to the abolitionists all they could hope at this time, and would surrender all the outworks by which the slaveholding States can defend their rights and property HERE, then a unanimous rejection of these petitions ought of right to follow."[3]

In Calhoun's opinion, Congress possessed no lawful power to limit slavery anywhere, not even within the geographical confines of Washington DC. He held fast to this view despite the inconvenient fact that Article I of the Constitution granted Congress the authority "to exercise exclusive legislation in all Cases whatsoever, over . . . the seat of the Government of the United States." Calhoun's principal argument, however, was not so much legal as it was political. Indeed, it was basically a naked political calculation. If the abolitionists succeeded in getting Congress to debate the merits of abolishing slavery in the District of Columbia, he reasoned, then it would only be a matter of time before Congress got around to debating the merits of abolishing slavery in the states. And for Calhoun, that outcome was to be prevented at all costs.

"No one can believe that the fanatics, who have flooded this and the other House with their petitions, entertain the slightest hope that Congress would pass a law *at this time* to abolish slavery in the District," Calhoun observed. So "what then do they hope?" Simply this: that Congress should "take jurisdiction of the subject" and "throw open to the abolitionists the halls of legislation and enable them to take a permanent position." At that point, "the subject of slavery would be agitated session after session" in Congress, "and from hence the assaults on the property and institutions of the people of the slaveholding States would be disseminated, in the guise of speeches, over the whole Union."[4]

Calhoun was a crafty politician, but he was also an accomplished intellectual. He recognized, perhaps as well as any thinker at the time, the very real danger that the abolitionist message posed for the slave system. "The war which the abolitionists wage against us is of a very different character, and far more effective" than merely shouldering a rifle and firing a shot, he argued. "It is a war of religious and political fanaticism," he observed, "waged not against our lives but our character. The object is to humble and debase us in our own estimation, and that of the world in general; to blast our reputation, while they overthrow our domestic institutions."[5] It is no wonder why Calhoun fought so desperately to silence the abolitionist petitions sent to Congress; he feared that the mere act of debating slavery would be a deadly loss for his side.

To say the least, Frederick Douglass and John C. Calhoun disagreed about a great many things. Yet on this particular point, the two men had reached remarkably similar conclusions. They both recognized the explosive force of abolitionist ideas, and they both believed that the abolitionist message, if allowed to spread far and wide, would do lasting damage to both the institution of slavery and to the standing of the slaveholding class. The only difference was that Douglass welcomed those results and did everything in his power to bring them about.

"Mr. John C. Calhoun, the great Southern statesman of the United States," Douglass would scoff, "stands upon the floor of the senate, and actually boasts that he is a robber!" Indeed, Calhoun "positively makes his boast of this disgraceful fact, and assigns it as a reason why he should be listened to as a man of consequence—a person of great importance. All his pretensions are founded upon the fact of his being a slaveowner. The audacity of these men," Douglass marveled, "is actually astounding."[6]

From the outset of his career as an abolitionist, Douglass had made it his mission to undermine the slaveholders and to expose the rank inhumanity of their system. Throughout his speeches and writings, for example, he would describe not only the places where he was held in bondage but also the people who kept him there. He named names. But as time wore on, Douglass began yearning to do much more than that. "It did not entirely satisfy me to *narrate* wrongs," he would write. "I felt like *denouncing* them."[7] In short, Douglass not only wanted to lay bare the villainous behavior of the slaveholders, but he also wanted to dissect and refute their flawed intellectual justifications. He wanted to destroy slavery while simultaneously making the case for liberty.

Once he got started, Douglass excelled at the job. In response to the elaborate rationales offered by Calhoun and other proslavery intellectuals, Douglass presented his own stirring defense of freedom, rooting his arguments in the bedrock liberal principle of self-ownership. "Would you have me argue that man is entitled to liberty? That he is the rightful owner of his own body?" Douglass would insist. "There is not a man beneath the canopy of heaven, that does not know that slavery is wrong *for him*."[8] At the same time, in response to the proslavery rulings of the American judiciary, such as Chief Justice Roger Taney's notorious 1857 opinion in *Dred Scott v. Sandford*, Douglass would deliver his own cutting legal analysis, forcefully rebutting "this hell-black judgment of the Supreme Court."[9]

Armed with the Constitution and the Declaration of Independence, and the far-reaching guarantees of liberty and equality that they contained, Frederick Douglass would take the fight directly to the slaveholders.

"A Positive Good"

Slavery's defenders put forward a variety of justifications in support of the peculiar institution. One such justification, commonly heard during the early decades of the republic, was that slavery was a necessary evil. As Congressman James Holland told the House of Representatives in 1806, "In the Southern States slavery is generally considered as a political evil, and in that point of view nearly all are disposed to stop the trade for the future."[10] Thomas Jefferson would express a similar view in an 1820 letter to the politician John Holmes. "The cessation of that kind of property," Jefferson wrote, referring to slavery, "would not cost me a second thought, if, in that way, a general emancipation and expatriation could be effected. . . . But as it is, we have the wolf by the ears, and we can neither hold him, nor safely let him go."[11]

But nobody ever heard John C. Calhoun describe slavery as any kind of evil. "Let me be not misunderstood as admitting, even by implication, that the existing relations between the two races in the slave-holding States is an evil—far otherwise," Calhoun would declare.[12] "The relation now existing in the slave-holding States between the two, is, instead of an evil, a good—a positive good."[13]

Unlike those members of the founding generation, such as the Virginia slaveowner George Mason, who acknowledged slavery's debasing influence on both master and slave, and therefore worked to partially limit slavery's influence on the new national government, Calhoun claimed that the system was a blessing all around and even argued that the slaves should be grateful for their chains. "The existing relations between the two races," Calhoun said, "is indispensable to the peace and happiness of both."[14]

As for the Constitution, Calhoun argued that it should never be used for any sort of antislavery purpose at all. "The North and South stand in the relation of partners in a common Union, with equal dignity and equal rights," he maintained.[15] And in order to maintain the South's equal dignity and rights, the argument went, slavery must be allowed to thrive with zero federal interference. Thus, in Calhoun's view, "Congress has no power whatever to prevent the citizens of the Southern States from emigrating with their property into the territories of the United States." Furthermore, as a corollary to that, "neither the inhabitants of the territories nor their legislatures have any such right" to stop the spread of slavery.[16] In other words, according to Calhoun, Congress did not even possess the authority to regulate slavery in those areas that were under the exclusive control of the federal government; nor did Congress have the right to recognize any new state that banned slavery within its own borders; nor did the settlers of any would-be state have any antislavery powers in their own hands. Slavery, Calhoun declared, must be permanently shielded on every front.

And that was not all. The only way to avoid secession and save the Union, Calhoun told the Senate in 1850, would be for the North to agree "to cease the agitation of the slave question, and to provide for the insertion of a provision in the Constitution, by an amendment, which will restore to the South, in substance, the power she possessed of protecting herself, before the equilibrium between the two sections was destroyed."[17] Put differently, Calhoun wanted to rewrite the Constitution in order to permanently safeguard—in fact, to prioritize—the interests of the slaveholders.

Unsurprisingly, Calhoun's audacious constitutional scheme attracted the notice of Frederick Douglass. Writing in the *North Star* a few days after the South Carolinian proposed rewriting the Constitution, Douglass mocked Calhoun's plan, labeling it an act of pure desperation. "The master-spirit of the South, the great champion of human bondage," Douglass wrote, was now grasping at straws. Calhoun knew that "a deep conviction of the sin of slavery" was growing among the American people, and he also knew that this conviction "could not long rest under the restraints, nor long abide what are called the compromises of the Constitution."[18] As a result, "Mr. Calhoun proposes an amendment of the Constitution!" How "lame and impotent." He "must amend, or rather deform," if his side is to prevail. What Calhoun's speech revealed, Douglass argued, was that the slave power was finally being thrown back on the defensive. To be sure, there were still many hard fights ahead, but "abolitionists can desire no stronger evidence of the efficiency of their measures," Douglass concluded, "than is given them in the speech of the great South Carolinian."[19] The exchange also revealed something else: Douglass was now going toe-to-toe with slavery's greatest champions, and the blows he delivered were leaving their mark.

"All Men Are Created Equal"

There was also the Declaration of Independence to factor in. Was not the entire American system founded on the "self-evident" truth that "all men are created equal" and endowed with "certain unalienable rights," such as "life, liberty, and the pursuit of happiness"? Did not that noble language vanquish the case for slavery?

Calhoun had wondered about that too. Sitting at his desk, Calhoun would ponder the Declaration's implications for his beloved slave system. In 1848 he finally followed his proslavery logic to its conclusion and denounced both the Declaration and its author, Thomas Jefferson. In fact, Calhoun went even further than that. He denounced the entire liberal tradition dating back to the English political theorist John Locke, who famously argued that government was instituted for the purpose of protecting humanity's pre-existing natural rights.

The notion that "all men are created equal," Calhoun declared, is "the most false and dangerous of all political errors."[20] It originated with "certain writers on government who had attained much celebrity in the early settlement of these States."[21] The most prominent of those writers was Locke, who preached the virtues of "that unbounded and individual liberty supposed to belong to man."[22] In Calhoun's view, Locke's liberal philosophy was dead wrong. "The quantum of power on the part of the government," Calhoun wrote, "instead of being equal in all cases, must necessarily be very unequal among different people, according to their different conditions." As for "individual liberty, or freedom," it "must be subordinate to whatever power may be necessary to protect society against anarchy within or destruction without." In short, "the safety and well-being of society," Calhoun declared, is necessarily "paramount to individual liberty."[23]

According to Calhoun, the great mistake of the American Revolution was that Locke's false theory of individual liberty "was inserted in our Declaration of Independence without any necessity. It made no necessary part of our justification in separating from the parent country." The impact of this mistake was not immediately felt. "For a long time it lay dormant," Calhoun wrote, "but in the process of time it began to germinate, and produce its poisonous fruits." Among those "poisonous fruits" was the rise of an abolitionist movement that took the language of the Declaration of Independence seriously and thus sought to overturn the slave system. Locke's fallacious notion of liberty "had strong hold on the mind of Mr. Jefferson," Calhoun complained, "which caused him to take an utterly false view of the subordinate relation of the black to the white race in the South; and to hold, in consequence, that the latter, though utterly unqualified to possess liberty, were as fully entitled to both liberty and equality as the former."[24]

Frederick Douglass had reached a similar conclusion—minus the racism and white supremacy. What is more, Douglass would do precisely what Calhoun feared: weaponize the principles of the Declaration of Independence and unleash them against slavery. "I am called, by way of reproach, a runaway slave," Douglass would say. "As if it were a crime—an unpardonable crime—for a man to take his inalienable rights!"[25]

Douglass would even enlist Jefferson's ghost in the antislavery crusade. In his 1784 *Notes on the State of Virginia*, Jefferson had shuddered at the prospects of a slave revolt against the master class, of which he himself was a part. "The Almighty has no attribute which can take side with us in such a contest," Jefferson admitted. "I tremble for my country when I reflect that God is just; that his justice cannot sleep forever."[26] Douglass would quote those very words in an 1850 speech on the inhumanity of slavery. "Such is the warning voice of Thomas Jefferson," Douglass observed. "Every day's experience since its utterance until now, confirms its wisdom, and commends its truth."[27]

"You Are a Man, and So Am I"

In 1854 the Virginia writer George Fitzhugh published the book that would make his name. *Sociology for the South, or The Failure of Free Society* offered a sweeping historical, political, and economic defense of the slave system. "The ancients took it for granted that slavery was right," Fitzhugh wrote, "and never attempted to justify it."[28] He attempted it; his efforts made him an acclaimed author throughout the slaveholding states.

Fitzhugh was born in Prince William County, Virginia, in 1806. His principal line of work was that of a lawyer, though it was only after he took up his pen as a polemicist that he found his true calling. "For thirty years the South has been a field on which abolitionists, foreign and domestic, have carried on offensive warfare," he wrote in *Sociology for the South*. "Let us now, in turn, act on the offensive, transfer the seat of war, and invade the enemies' territory."[29]

Fitzhugh was unapologetically, unconditionally proslavery. "Men are not 'born entitled to equal rights!'" Fitzhugh declared. "It would be far nearer the truth to say, 'that some were born with saddles on their backs, and others booted and spurred to ride them.'—and the riding does them good."[30]

Fitzhugh's strident arguments quickly attracted notice throughout the United States. "It is very satisfactory to find the justification of the South is no longer limited to excuses, expediencies, dialectics, rhetoric, verbal quibbles and vain enactments," raved the *Southern Literary Messenger* in its review of the book, "but is at length planted on the firm basis of philosophical reasoning, historical testimony, and social experience." Fitzhugh's *Sociology for the South*, that paper told its readers, "should be in the hands of every Southern man."[31] Abraham Lincoln, who was then practicing law in Illinois, also picked up a copy of Fitzhugh's work. According to his law partner, William Herndon, Lincoln read *Sociology for the South* with keen interest. Fitzhugh "defended slavery in every way," Herndon reported. "This aroused the ire of Lincoln more than most pro-slavery books."[32]

Like Calhoun, Fitzhugh sneered at Thomas Jefferson, denouncing him for penning "that bombastic absurdity in our Declaration of Independence about the inalienable rights of man."[33] Fitzhugh also sneered at John Locke and the natural-rights tradition that he had helped to found. "We believe no heresy in moral science has been more pregnant of mischief than this theory of Locke," Fitzhugh wrote. "[Man] has no rights whatever, as opposed to the interests of society; and that society may very properly make any use of him that will redound to the public good." Indeed, Fitzhugh insisted, "whatever rights he has are subordinate to the good of the whole; and he has never ceded rights to it, for he was born its slave, and had no rights to cede."[34]

Writing in 1863, Fitzhugh would argue that the Civil War ultimately came about due to the confrontation between two fundamentally opposing principles, those of liberalism and of slavery. "The doctrines of Jefferson and of the illustrious fathers of the Republic, were being successfully employed to justify abolition," he observed. That is what sparked "the Southern Revolution of 1861," which Fitzhugh described as "a solemn protest against the doctrines of natural liberty, human equality and the social contract as taught by Locke and the American sages of 1776, and an equally solemn protest against the doctrines of Adam Smith . . . and the rest of the infidel, political economists, who maintain that the world is too much governed, '*Pas trop gouverner*' and should not be governed at all, but, 'Let alone,' '*Laissez nous faire*.'"[35]

Frederick Douglass also understood that slavery and liberalism were fundamentally incompatible. Locke, in his 1681 book, *The Second Treatise of Government*, had argued that "every man has a property in his own person. This nobody has any right to but himself."[36] Douglass did more than just take those words to heart; he used them as the foundation for an all-out attack on the slave system. In his writings and speeches, Douglass would champion the very liberal principles that Fitzhugh and Calhoun had spurned.

"Every man is the *original, natural, rightful,* and *absolute* owner of his own body," Douglass argued, "and he can only part from *his* self-ownership, by the commission of a crime."[37] In other words, slavery only existed because the slaveholders relied on violence, theft, and intimidation to maintain their criminal control over the bodies of the enslaved. Such actions violated every principle of the natural-rights philosophy—and the slaveholders knew it. That was why proslavery thinkers like Calhoun and Fitzhugh were forced to explicitly repudiate Locke, Jefferson, and the Declaration of Independence.

Douglass made the case for natural rights with particular force on September 3, 1848, when he wrote an open letter to his former master, the slaveholder Thomas Auld. Douglass began by stating "the ground upon which I justify myself . . . to mention your name in public." Undoubtedly, he observed, some people "will be shocked by the extremely indelicate manner of bringing your name before" the eyes of the world. So why was Douglass doing it? "A man guilty of theft, robbery, or murder," he told the slaveholder, "has forfeited the right to concealment and private life."[38]

Douglass then got down to business. Since escaping from Auld's control ten years earlier, he wrote, "I have often thought I should like to explain to you the grounds upon which I have justified myself in running away from you." The justification was simple. "You are a man, and so am I. . . . In leaving you, I took nothing but what belonged to me, and in no way lessened your means for obtaining an *honest* living. Your faculties remained yours, and mine became useful to their rightful owner."[39]

It was the natural-rights philosophy in a nutshell: self-ownership, personal liberty, individualism. Although he is not normally credited as such, Frederick Douglass undoubtedly deserves to be ranked as one of the nineteenth century's foremost proponents of Lockean liberalism.

"This Fourth of July Is Yours, Not Mine"

Frederick Douglass delivered perhaps his greatest defense of liberal principles on July 5, 1852. He was just thirty-four years old that day, and fourteen years out of bondage, as he stood before five hundred to six hundred mostly white people in Rochester, New York, at the grand Corinthian Hall, where he was scheduled to commemorate the anniversary of American independence with a speech titled "What to the Slave Is the Fourth of July?"

The event was organized by the Rochester Ladies Anti-Slavery Society, a group that had formed the previous year in order to promote "the diffusion of Anti-Slavery Sentiments by means of the Press and Lecturer; to the relief of the suffering Fugitive, and for such other Anti-Slavery objects as may present itself." The society was ostensibly organized as a big tent, welcoming antislavery activists of all stripes, while taking no official side in the bitter fights, both factional and philosophical, that divided the various abolitionist camps. Yet as the historian Leigh Fought has pointed out, "despite this insistence on neutrality, however, the very language of the Rochester Ladies' constitution placed them in direct opposition to one of the central tenets of Garrisonian abolition." Namely, the group supported constitutional action against slavery. The U.S. Constitution "was adopted by the *People* of the United States to establish *Justice*, provide for the *common Defense*, insure *Domestic Tranquility*, and secure to themselves and posterity the blessing of *Liberty*," the group observed in its charter. The institution of slavery, by "depriving one portion of the people of the inestimable blessings of Liberty, is a gross violation of Justice, and greatly endangers the Domestic Tranquility."[40] Put differently, Douglass would be delivering his Fourth of July oration before a large, ideologically friendly crowd in his recently adopted hometown.

He began his speech innocently enough, taking note of the great civic occasion that brought them all together. "The 4th of July is the first great fact in your nation's history," he observed. "The Declaration of Independence is the ringbolt to the chain of your nation's destiny."[41] He then offered a brief, positive sketch of the American Revolution.

But that respectful tone was soon replaced by a stern voice of anger and reproach. "What have I, or those I represent, to do with your national independence?" Douglass asked. "Are the great principles of political freedom and of natural justice, embodied in the Declaration of Independence, extended to us?"[42] Of course not, and everyone present knew it—a bitter fact that he proceeded to drive home. After sharply contrasting "your Fourth of July" with the miseries of the American slave, Douglass informed his audience that "this Fourth of July is *yours*, not *mine. You* may rejoice, *I* must mourn."[43]

Describing the outrages that he both witnessed and endured during his twenty years in bondage, Douglass proceeded to paint a bleak, horrific portrait of the slave system. Consider the domestic slave trade, he told the crowd. "Attend the auction," he said. "See men examined like horses; see the forms of women rudely and brutally exposed to the shocking gaze of American slave-buyers. See this drove sold and separated forever; and never forget the deep, sad sobs that arose from that scattered multitude." And this, he made clear, was no work of fiction, no imaginary tale. "I was born amid such sights and scenes."[44]

Now consider the Fugitive Slave Act of 1850, Douglass continued. That notorious law effectively removed all legal protections from suspected runaways, including their right to trial by jury, their right to present evidence in their own defense, and their right to petition the courts for a writ of habeas corpus. As a direct result, both runaway slaves and free blacks had been snatched off the streets and turned over to the control of the slavers. Even worse, when an alleged fugitive was brought before a government commissioner under the 1850 law, that commissioner would receive ten dollars for every person "returned" to slavery yet receive just five dollars for every person that was set free, thereby tilting the outcome directly in favor of slavery. "The seats of justice are filled with judges who hold their offices under an open and palpable *bribe*," Douglass scorned, "and are bound, in deciding the case of a man's liberty, *to hear only his accusers!*"[45]

For Douglass, this part of the speech was no mere intellectual discussion. Not only was he a former fugitive slave himself, but he was also an active contributor to the vast network of safe houses and escape routes known as the Underground Railroad. Given its proximity to the Canadian border, Douglass's adopted hometown of Rochester was the last stop for many escapees on their route to freedom. And Douglass himself was well known for welcoming such travelers to his own residence, raising money on their behalf, and helping them decamp to Canada. "The secrecy of the Underground Railroad makes it impossible to determine the number of slaves Douglass aided," one historian has noted. "But it was a figure which easily ran into the hundreds."[46] In 1851, for example, Douglass opened his home to a man named William Parker, a free black man traveling with two escaped slaves. Parker had previously sheltered the two runaways at his own home in Pennsylvania, but their owner, accompanied by U.S. marshals, showed up one day, sparking a violent confrontation in which the owner was killed. The three then fled farther north, ultimately arriving in Rochester, where Douglass helped to make good their escape to Canada. "The slave is a man and ought not to be treated like a horse," Douglass wrote of Parker and his confederates. "And his manhood is his justification for shooting down any creature who shall attempt to reduce him to the condition of a brute."[47]

Douglass made no attempt to hide his disgust at the many evils he was describing in his Fourth of July oration. "I do not hesitate to declare," he said, "with all my soul, that the character and conduct of this nation never looked blacker to me than on this 4th of July!"[48]

In many ways, Douglass employed the same style of scathing, damning rhetoric so often heard from the lips of his former mentor, William Lloyd Garrison, who had denounced the very founding of the United States as an atrocious compact with evil. Much like Garrison himself would have done in the same situation, Douglass treated the Fourth of July as the perfect occasion to rain down hellfire and brimstone on the sins of slaveholding America.

But while Garrison was known to conclude such speeches by setting fire to a copy of the U.S. Constitution, Douglass was building toward a very different type of crescendo that day in Rochester. To be clear, he announced, "there is not a nation on the earth guilty of practices, more shocking and bloody, than are the people of the United States, at this very hour."[49] Still, Douglass refused to forsake America's founding principles, no matter how far the country had strayed in practice. His objective was to save America from the corrupting influence of slavery, and as he made clear, he would accomplish this goal by restoring the nation to what he saw as its original, liberty-minded purposes.

Douglass did so by first drawing explicit parallels between the courageous signers of the Declaration of Independence—men who "preferred revolution to peaceful submission to bondage"—and the brave abolitionists struggling to end slavery in the present. When it came to the founding fathers, Douglass said, "nothing was 'settled' that was not right. With them, justice, liberty, and humanity were 'final': not slavery and oppression."[50] That description applied equally well to Douglass himself.

At the same time, Douglass also embraced the natural-rights philosophy on which the Declaration of Independence was based. For example, evoking John Locke's famous description of private property emerging from man mixing his labor with the natural world, Douglass pointed to slaves "plowing, planting and reaping, using all kinds of mechanical tools, erecting houses," as proof that they, too, deserved the full range of natural rights.[51] "Am I to argue that it is wrong to make men brutes, to rob them of their liberty, to strip them of their wages . . . to starve them into obedience and submission to their masters?" Douglass demanded of his mostly white audience. "No!" Douglass thundered.[52] The humanity of black Americans was not up for debate. The wrongs of slavery were beyond self-evident.

Finally, turning to the Constitution, Douglass characterized it as both the founding generation's greatest achievement and the abolitionists' greatest weapon. "There is no matter in respect to which the people of the North have allowed themselves to be so ruinously imposed upon as that of the pro-slavery character of the Constitution," he declared. Where is this so-called support for slavery to be found? Is it in the Preamble, which lays out the document's overarching commitment to liberty and justice? Is it in the main body, which contains neither the word *slave* nor the word *slavery*? "I hold there is neither warrant, license, nor sanction of the hateful thing," Douglass told the crowd. Rather, "interpreted, as it ought to be interpreted, the Constitution is a glorious liberty document."[53]

Douglass spoke for several hours that day, and his remarks would be justly remembered as one of the greatest speeches of his long career. "Notwithstanding the dark picture I have this day presented," he concluded, "I do not despair of this country. There are forces in operation which must inevitably work the downfall of slavery."[54]

Five years later, the U.S. Supreme Court would put Douglass's constitutional faith to the test when it issued Chief Justice Roger B. Taney's notorious and far-reaching decision in the case of *Dred Scott v. Sandford*.

"Looked Upon as Citizens"

Here is a surprising fact about the arch proslavery jurist Roger Brooke Taney: During his days as a trial lawyer, Taney once defended the rights of an abolitionist minister and told a Maryland jury that slavery was an "evil" that should be abolished. Taney was born in 1777 to a family of slaveholding tobacco farmers in Calvert County, Maryland. In 1818 he crossed paths with Reverend Jacob Gruber. That year, Gruber, a Methodist from Pennsylvania, had spoken out against the "inhuman traffic and cruel trade" of slavery, before a large religious gathering in Hagerstown, Maryland. "Is it not a reproach to man to hold articles of liberty and independence in one hand," Gruber asked the crowd, "and a bloody whip in the other, while a negro stands and trembles before him, with his back cut and bleeding?"[55]

The local authorities did not exactly appreciate that kind of talk. Indeed, they proceeded to bring Gruber up on charges of attempting to incite a slave revolt. Taney, a prominent local lawyer, took the case and defended Gruber at trial. "I need not tell you," Taney told the jury, "that, by the liberal and happy institutions of this State, the rights of conscience and the freedom of speech are fully protected. No man can be prosecuted for preaching the articles of his religious creed."[56]

It was a straightforward defense based on neutral principles of free speech. But then Taney went further. "A hard necessity," he continued in his remarks to the jury, "compels us to endure the evil of slavery for a time." And so long as this evil persists, he declared, "it is a blot on our national character; and every real lover of freedom confidently hopes that it will be effectually, though it must be gradually, wiped away."[57] The jury apparently liked what it heard and delivered a not guilty verdict for Taney's client.

Here is another surprising fact: Taney refused to own slaves himself. "I am not a slaveholder," he would write in an 1857 letter. "More than thirty years ago I manumitted every slave I ever owned, except two, who were too old, when they became my property, to provide for themselves. These two I supported in comfort as long as they lived."[58] And so he did. Taney inherited a number of slaves from his family during his young adulthood; he set them all free, minus only the exceptions he mentioned in that letter.

But let us not paint too rosy a picture here of the future chief justice. Whatever personal qualms he may or may not have harbored regarding the institution of slavery, Taney, when it came to his long and influential career on the national stage, would emerge as nothing less than one of the greatest defenders of slavery in all of American history.

Consider Taney's actions while serving as attorney general of the United States during the administration of President Andrew Jackson. In 1831 Charles Bankhead, the British chargé d'affaires in Washington DC, filed a complaint with the U.S. secretary of state Edward Livingston about the treatment of black British sailors at the hands of local authorities in South Carolina. According to the laws of that state, all free black sailors had to be jailed while their respective vessels were docked in the state's ports and harbors. Those sailors were only set free once their ships were ready to leave and their captains showed up to pay for the costs of their imprisonment. If nobody showed up to pay, the free blacks were sold into slavery.

Unsurprisingly, Bankhead was aghast at such treatment of his country's sailors, viewing it as a gross violation of the treaty between Great Britain and the United States. As he informed Secretary of State Livingston, he objected to "the power of a state to make any law which has for its object the forcible detention of British subjects, under circumstances altogether at variance with the freedom of commercial intercourse between nations, and unauthorized by any treaty or convention."[59]

Before replying, Livingston asked Attorney General Taney for his legal opinion on the matter. In essence, the question for Taney was this: Did the U.S. treaty with Great Britain trump the lawmaking powers of South Carolina in this instance and therefore require the state to stop jailing free black sailors? In reply, Taney maintained that no federal treaty (and no federal law) could trump the reserved lawmaking powers of a state, particularly when it came to a state's regulatory authority over its black residents and visitors. The British were out of luck.

To support his position, Taney laid out a fundamentally racist vision of American law, one that placed blacks in a permanently subordinate position. "The African race in the United States, even when free, are everywhere a degraded class," Taney told the secretary of state. "The privileges they are allowed to enjoy, are accorded to them as a matter of kindness and benevolence rather than of right." In fact, "they were never regarded as a constituent portion of any state" and "were not looked upon as citizens by the contracting parties who formed the Constitution."[60] In effect, Taney maintained, blacks could never possess the same rights and privileges as whites.

As for the Declaration of Independence and its well-known language proclaiming liberty as the inalienable birthright of all, Taney effectively rewrote that document to make it read "for whites only." "No one ever supposed that the African race in this country were entitled to the benefit of this declaration," Taney asserted, "nor did any one imagine that they had a right to claim the extension of that great privilege to themselves."[61]

It was a foul taste of things to come. Twenty-five years later, while serving as chief justice of the United States, Taney would express that same view, in even blunter terms, while deciding the fate of the slave Dred Scott. The black man, Taney would write, in what would go down as perhaps the single most infamous sentence in American legal history, "has no rights which the white man was bound to respect."[62]

"Once Free, Forever Free"

The landmark case of *Dred Scott v. Sandford* originated in 1833 when an army doctor named John Emerson purchased an enslaved man named Dred Scott in St. Louis, Missouri. Over the following decade, Emerson's job took him and his new slave to various places around the country. Between 1833 and 1836 the two resided at Fort Armstrong, which was located in the free state of Illinois. Between 1836 and 1838 they resided in Fort Snelling, located in the present-day state of Minnesota, which was then still part of the territory acquired from France in the Louisiana Purchase of 1803. According to the terms of the 1820 federal law known as the Missouri Compromise, under which Maine entered the Union as a free state while Missouri entered as a slave state, slavery was prohibited "in all that territory ceded by France to the United States, under the name of Louisiana, which lies north of thirty-six degrees and thirty minutes north latitude, not included within the limits of the state" of Missouri.[63] Fort Snelling—which sat north of the thirty-six, thirty line—was therefore designated as free territory by Congress.

In 1846, back in the slave state of Missouri, Scott attempted to buy his freedom, as well as that of his wife, Harriet, and their two children, from John Emerson's widow, Irene Emerson, after the doctor had died in 1843. After she refused to sell, Scott initiated the legal proceedings that would eventually add his name to the annals of American history.

Dred Scott had a powerful legal argument on his side; when a master took a slave to live on free soil, the master emancipated that slave. As the historian Don E. Fehrenbacher has written, "Once the subject of a suit for freedom was raised, anyone familiar with Missouri law could have told the Scotts that they had a very strong case. Again and again, the highest court of the state had ruled that a master who took his slave to reside in a state or territory where slavery was prohibited thereby emancipated him."[64] For example, in the 1824 case of *Winny v. Whitesides*, the Missouri Supreme Court recognized the freedom of a slave who had been taken to live in the free state of Illinois, the very place where Scott had been taken to live in 1833. Likewise, in the 1836 case of *Rachel v. Walker*, the Missouri Supreme Court recognized the freedom of a slave who had been taken to live at Fort Snelling, in the free Louisiana Territory, the very place where Scott had been taken to live in 1836. In legal circles, this was known as the doctrine of "once free, forever free."

But when Scott's case finally reached the Missouri Supreme Court in 1852, that body defied expectations by disregarding its own precedents and reaching an entirely different conclusion. The antislavery laws of Illinois "have no intrinsic right to be enforced beyond the limits of the State for which they were enacted," declared Judge William Scott. "The respect allowed them will depend altogether on their conformity to the policy of our institutions."[65] In short, the fact that Dr. Emerson had taken Dred Scott to live in a free state or territory no longer carried any weight before that tribunal.

What explained the state high court's extraordinary legal turnaround? According to Judge Scott, the outcome of the case had little to do with legal precedent and everything to do with protecting slavery. "On almost three sides, the State of Missouri is surrounded by free soil," Judge Scott wrote. If Dred Scott prevailed, that would mean that "if one of our slaves touch that soil with his master's ascent, he becomes entitled to his freedom."[66] For Judge Scott, that outcome was intolerable.

The Missouri judge frankly acknowledged that his decision turned the court's earlier rulings upside down. But "times now are not as they were, when the former decisions on this subject were made," he wrote. "Since then not only individuals but States have been possessed with a dark and fell spirit in relation to slavery, whose gratification is sought in the pursuit of measures whose inevitable consequence must be the overthrow and destruction of our government."[67] In other words, because abolitionist sentiment was on the rise, Missouri must double down in its defense of the peculiar institution, and the state's high court must refuse to do anything that might give aid or comfort to the antislavery cause.

At this point, for reasons that are not entirely clear, Dred Scott's legal team shifted tactics. Rather than appeal the state court loss to the U.S. Supreme Court, a new case was filed in federal court. In effect, there would be two different Dred Scott cases. The first, *Scott v. Emerson*, culminated with Scott's 1852 loss at the Missouri Supreme Court. The second, *Scott v. Sandford*, went all the way up to the highest court in the land.

The key difference between them was that in the federal case, Scott, a resident of Missouri, was suing John Sanford, a resident of New York, who was the brother of Irene Emerson and the executor of John Emerson's estate. Because the court reporter misspelled Sanford's name, the case went down on the books as *Scott v. Sandford* and has remained so misnamed ever since.

The federal dispute centered on three legal questions, each one of momentous importance, not only for the parties involved, but for the entire nation. First, did free blacks (as Scott claimed to be) qualify as U.S. citizens with standing to sue in federal court? Second, was Scott made free when Dr. Emerson took him to live at Fort Snelling, which was designated as free territory by Congress under the Missouri Compromise? And third, did Congress actually possess the constitutional authority to outlaw slavery in the federal territories in the first place, or was the Missouri Compromise itself unconstitutional?

In his brief for the plaintiff, Scott's lawyer, Montgomery Blair, stressed to the Supreme Court that while there may be a "recognized social distinction" between free blacks and whites in some parts of the country, this distinction did not alter the fact that free blacks routinely exercised the basic rights associated with citizenship, such as "suing and being sued," "holding property," and enjoying "the right to trial by jury, to the writ of habeas corpus, or to any right or privilege essential to the enjoyment of their liberty and property."[68] Indeed, he pointed out, the Constitution "recognized but two kinds of free persons—citizens and aliens;—nobody supposes that free negroes are aliens; they are, therefore, necessarily citizens, and are, in fact, so regarded and treated."[69]

As for the constitutionality of the Missouri Compromise, Blair wrote, "this is a question of more importance, perhaps, than any which was ever submitted to this court ... it is, indeed, the great question of our day and time."[70] It dealt with nothing less than whether America would be "a free or slave continent."[71] The idea that Congress possessed the lawful power to outlaw slavery in the federal territories, Blair insisted, was firmly established by both legal precedent and government practice. The very first Congress, he noted, passed legislation enforcing the Northwest Ordinance of 1787, which outlawed slavery in the federal territory that was north and west of the Ohio River. Surely, he maintained, that was more than sufficient evidence of Congress's long-standing lawful power in this area. "If the policy of extending slavery be assented to," Blair told the justices, "the era of the founders has passed."[72]

H. S. Geyer, the lawyer for John Sanford, took the opposite view on every point. "Free blacks are not citizens within the provisions of the Constitution," he told the Supreme Court. As for Dred Scott, "a negro, born a slave," he "is not and cannot be a citizen of the State of Missouri."[73]

Turning next to Scott's claim to freedom under federal law, Geyer dismissed the Missouri Compromise as a lawless act of federal overreach. "No residence of a slave at Fort Snelling could change his condition or divest the title of his owner," Geyer maintained. "Slavery existed by law in all the territory ceded by France to the United States, and Congress has not the constitutional power to repeal that law, or abolish or prohibit slavery within any part of that territory."[74]

With the briefs filed and the legal battle lines drawn, the U.S. Supreme Court scheduled oral arguments in the case to commence on February 11, 1856.

"The Commanding and Vital Issue"

Scott v. Sandford arrived at the U.S. Supreme Court amid a loaded moment in American history. In 1854, Congress, bowing to proslavery pressure, had passed the sweeping federal law known as the Kansas-Nebraska Act. A partial repeal of the Missouri Compromise, this law allowed the settlers of the Kansas Territory to decide for themselves whether or not slavery would be allowed in that soon-to-be state. As a result, both pro- and antislavery forces had converged on the territory, each side hoping to swing the political outcome in favor of its preferred stance. Violent confrontations soon followed. In May 1856 one antislavery settler, the militant abolitionist John Brown, joined by seven other men, including four of his sons, massacred five proslavery settlers after dragging them at night from their homes near Pottawatomie Creek, Kansas. "Death for death," John Brown Jr. later explained.[75]

That same month, on the floor of the U.S. Senate, Senator Charles Sumner of Massachusetts was beaten senseless while sitting at his desk by a cane-wielding South Carolina congressman named Preston Brooks. A few days earlier, Sumner had delivered a lengthy denunciation of both the Kansas-Nebraska Act and the spread of slavery into free-soil territory. Sumner had also singled out a few politicians for special abuse. Among them was Senator Andrew Butler of South Carolina, who, Sumner declared, had "chosen a mistress to whom he . . . made his vows, and who, though ugly to others, [was] always lovely to him . . . the harlot, Slavery."[76] Representative Brooks was the younger cousin of Senator Butler. "I felt it to be my duty to relieve Butler," Brooks declared after his assault on Sumner, "and avenge the insult to my State."[77] It would be several years before Sumner fully recovered from the vicious head wounds that he received that day.

Meanwhile, in that same busy year, 1856, Democratic president Franklin Pierce, who had signed the Kansas-Nebraska Act into law two years earlier, informed Congress that, in his view, the national legislature "does not possess constitutional power" to impose any restriction whatsoever on slavery in "any present or future State of the Union."[78] According to the president of the United States, in other words, the Missouri Compromise had been illegal all along and Congress was entirely powerless to stop the expansion of slavery into the federal territories.

"The extension or the limitation of Slavery," observed Frederick Douglass in an August 1856 editorial, is "the commanding and vital issue . . . at the approaching Presidential election."[79] The Democrats, of course, were totally worthless on the subject, having surrendered control of their party to the proslavery fanatics. The Whigs were equally worthless. Indeed, that party was on the verge of extinction; 1856 would be the last year in which the Whig Party held a national convention. But the new Republican Party, founded two years earlier on antislavery principles, was a different story. As a result, Douglass informed his readers, he would be throwing his full support in the coming national election behind the Republican presidential candidacy of John C. Frémont and his running mate, William L. Dayton, who were campaigning on the same platform that had recently animated the Free-Soilers: namely, Freedom National, Slavery Sectional. Frémont and Dayton are "the admitted and recognized antagonists of the Slave Power, of gag-law, and of all the hellish designs of the Slave Power to extend and fortify the accursed slave system."[80] The antislavery movement must unite with these Republicans, Douglass stressed, and preserve the constitutional power of Congress to prohibit slavery in the federal territories. "The point attacked, is the point to be defended. The South has tendered to us the issue of Slavery Extension; and to meet the Slave Power here . . . is to strike hardest, where the Slaveholders feel most keenly."[81]

Against this backdrop of violence, conflict, and political unrest, the U.S. Supreme Court was busy deliberating on the fate of Dred Scott.

"No Rights"

It was the morning of March 6, 1857, and Chief Justice Roger Taney was about to make history. Did he understand the importance of what he was about to do? There is some reason to think that he did.

The debate over slavery was reaching a boiling point. Violent attacks between pro- and antislavery advocates were breaking out not only in the rough-hewn territory of Kansas but in the hallowed halls of Congress. And in the eyes of many Americans, the U.S. Supreme Court was seen as perhaps the last, best hope for a peaceable solution that both sides might agree to abide. Taney, an accomplished and arrogant man, undoubtedly believed that his judgment had the power to settle once and for all the controversies over both black citizenship and the expansion of slavery. As it turned out, Taney's sweeping ruling in the case only added more fuel to the fire.

It took the chief justice some two hours to read his opinion from the bench that day. Surely, he noticed the unusually crowded courtroom packed full of both eager journalists and interested lay observers, all keenly following the crucial national issues at stake. Did he bother to notice that Dred Scott, the ostensible man of the hour, was absent from the chamber and was instead back in the slave state of Missouri, awaiting news of his fate? Had Scott been present, he would have witnessed the chief justice deliver what would go down as one of the most reviled rulings in American legal history.

"The question is simply this," Taney declared. "Can a negro, whose ancestors were imported into this country, and sold as slaves, become a member of the political community formed and brought into existence by the Constitution of the United States, and as such become entitled to all the rights, and privileges, and immunities, guaranteed by that instrument to the citizen?"[82]

Taney thought not. Blacks "are not included, and were not intended to be included, under the word 'citizens' in the Constitution." In fact, Taney asserted, at the time of the American founding, blacks "had for more than a century before been regarded as beings of an inferior order." They comprised no part of "We the People" and may only enjoy such fleeting privileges "as those who held the power and the Government might choose to grant them."[83]

As for the argument that Dred Scott was made free when his master took him to live in free federal territory, Taney responded that Congress entirely lacked the authority to designate any part of U.S. territory as free soil. If the slaveholders wanted, they could spread their peculiar institution far and wide. "It is the opinion of the court," Taney held, "that the act of Congress which prohibited a citizen from holding and owning property of this kind in the territory of the United States north of the [thirty-six, thirty line] is not warranted by the Constitution, and is therefore void."[84] Just as Congress may not restrict slavery in the states, Taney concluded, it may not restrict slavery in the territories. The Missouri Compromise, in other words, had just been ruled unconstitutional. So, too, had the Freedom National platform of the new Republican Party.

Writing in dissent, Justice Benjamin Curtis took aim at Taney's skewed historical narrative. Of course free blacks qualified as U.S. citizens, Curtis observed: "At the time of the ratification of the Articles of Confederation, all free native-born inhabitants of the States of New Hampshire, Massachusetts, New York, New Jersey, and North Carolina, though descended from African slaves, were not only citizens of those States, but such of them as had the other necessary qualifications possessed the franchise of electors, on equal terms with other citizens."[85]

As for the Constitution, Curtis wrote, it fully cemented the case for black citizenship. When the document was up for ratification, he noted, "in some of the States, as we have seen, colored persons were among those qualified by law to act on this subject. These colored persons were not only included in the body of 'the people of the United States,' by whom the Constitution was ordained and established, but in at least five of the States they had the power to act, and doubtless did act, by their suffrages, upon the question of its adoption." Put differently, in the historic years of 1787 and 1788, some of the very same people whom Taney was now retroactively excluding from U.S. citizenship were busy voting to bring the Constitution to life. "It would be strange," Curtis concluded, "if we were to find in that instrument anything which deprived of their citizenship any part of the people of the United States who were among those by whom it was established."[86]

It was a compelling dissent, carefully argued and firmly rooted in constitutional history—but it was still a dissent. Taney's racist judgment carried the day. According to the chief justice of the United

States, Dred Scott, along with every other black American, "had no rights which the white man was bound to respect."[87]

"This Devilish Decision"

To say that *Dred Scott* ignited a firestorm in American politics would be putting it mildly. The court's infernal judgment, declared Congressman Thaddeus Stevens of Pennsylvania, "damned [Taney] to everlasting fame; and, I fear, to everlasting fire."[88]

For Douglass, the court's opinion represented the antithesis of virtually everything he stood for. The issue of black citizenship, for instance, was of paramount importance to him—for obvious reasons. "I have a right to come into this State to prosecute any lawful business in a lawful manner," Douglass told a Chicago audience in 1854. "This is a natural right, and is a part of the supreme law of the land." Furthermore, "in the State of New York, where I live, I am a citizen and a legal voter, and may therefore be presumed to be a citizen of the United States." After all, the Constitution "knows no man by the color of his skin. . . . The word white is a modern term in the legislation of this country."[89]

Likewise, in a speech to the Colored National Convention in Rochester, New York, in 1853, Douglass laid out the case for black citizenship in careful detail. "By birth, we are American citizens," he observed. "By the principles of the Declaration of Independence, we are American citizens; within the meaning of the Constitution, we are American citizens."[90] The citizenship of black Americans was equally supported by historical practice. Do not forget, he told his audience, that black troops fought under General Andrew Jackson in the Battle of New Orleans during the War of 1812. Do they not count as Americans? What about Crispus Attucks, the runaway slave killed by the British at the Boston Massacre of 1770. Was he not among the first casualties of the American Revolution and thus one of the new nation's first martyred heroes?

On May 11, a little less than two months after the *Dred Scott* decision was announced, Douglass stood before a meeting of the American Anti-Slavery Society in New York City and addressed Taney's judgment at length. "To many, the prospects of the struggle against slavery seem far from cheering," he began.[91] Yet the future looked brighter when considered in light of the recent past. "Take this fact—for it is a fact—the anti-slavery movement has, from first to last, suffered no abatement. It has gone forth in all directions, and is now felt in the remotest extremities of the Republic." Yes, the movement had been censured, castigated, opposed. Yet still its ranks grew larger with each passing day. "Loud and exultingly have we been told that the slavery question is settled, and settled forever." But from the political landscape of the country, "the more the question has been settled," Douglass laughed, "the more it has needed settling."[92]

That brought him to the chief justice. The latest such attempt to settle the slavery question "must be called the Taney settlement."[93] Remarkably, Douglass observed, Taney seemed to think that his shrill voice might finally do the trick and silence the abolitionists for good. In point of fact, Douglass countered, "this very attempt to blot out forever the hopes of an enslaved people may be one necessary link in the chain of events preparatory to the downfall and complete overthrow of the whole slave system."[94] In a few years' time, with the *Dred Scott* decision emerging as one of the proximate causes of the Civil War, those words of Douglass's would come to seem almost prophetic.

Douglass then turned his full attention to "this devilish decision—this judicial incarnation of wolfishness."[95] Combining legal analysis with natural-rights theory, Douglass dissected Taney's opinion. "I have a quarrel with those who fling the Supreme Law of this land between the slave and freedom," he announced. Before "I admit that slavery is constitutional, I must see slavery recognized in the Constitution." Yet just look at the document. "Neither in the preamble nor in the body of the Constitution is there a single mention of the term *slave* or *slave holder, slave master* or *slave state*, neither is there any reference to the color, or the physical peculiarities of any part of the people of the United States."[96]

So where, Douglass demanded, will Taney "find a guarantee for slavery? Will he find it in the declaration that no person shall be deprived of life, liberty, or property, without due process of law? Will he find it in the declaration that the Constitution was established to secure the blessing of liberty? Will he find it in the right of the people to be secure in their persons and papers, and houses, and effects?" Any one of those constitutional provisions just named, Douglass said, if "faithfully carried out, would put an end to slavery in every State in the American Union."[97]

Douglass began his speech on *Dred Scott* by sounding a note of optimism, proclaiming his faith in the ultimate triumph of the abolitionist cause. But he also issued a fearsome note of warning to the slaveholding class. "Jefferson said that he trembled for his country when he reflected that God is just, and his justice cannot sleep forever," Douglass reminded them. "The time may come when even the crushed worm may turn under the tyrant's feet." Indeed, "the world is full of violence and fraud, and it would be strange," Douglass said, "if the slave, the constant victim of both fraud and violence, should escape the contagion. He, too, may learn to fight the devil with fire, and for one, I am in no frame of mind to pray that this may be long deferred."[98]

A little less than four years later, the opening shots of the Civil War rang out.

4

"Men of Color, to Arms!"

On April 12, 1861, Confederate general Pierre Gustave Toutant Beauregard, acting on orders from the man he called president, Jefferson Davis, gave the command to open fire on Fort Sumter, a U.S. military facility strategically located on a man-made island in the harbor of Charleston, South Carolina. With those shots, the Civil War was officially underway.

"God be praised!" Frederick Douglass cheered upon learning the news.[1] As far as Douglass was concerned, he, just like every other black American, had been at war with slavery for his entire life. During his twenty years in bondage, he had been flogged, beaten, and tortured. As a teenager, he had squared off against the feared "negro breaker" Edward Covey and drawn blood from his enemy. As a fugitive from slavery, he had risked life and limb escaping to freedom. As a conductor on the Underground Railroad, he had kept his eyes peeled for armed slave catchers. As an abolitionist orator, he had faced down racist mobs that were intent on doing him harm. The time was long overdue, Douglass believed, for the federal government to join the fight against the slave power.

Thankfully, the secessionists had just done the cause of antislavery a tremendous favor. By attacking Fort Sumter, Douglass wrote, they have "exposed the throat of slavery to the keen knife of liberty, and have given a chance to all the righteous forces of this nation to deal a death-blow to the monster evil of the nineteenth century."[2] Douglass had long implored the federal government to unleash its entire constitutional arsenal against the peculiar institution. Now he would urge one federal official in particular, President Abraham Lincoln, to exercise his considerable powers as commander in chief for that very same purpose. "The Government is active, and the people aroused," Douglass celebrated.[3] The great war for freedom was finally at hand.

Yet as the Civil War got going in earnest, the Union's tactics increasingly left Douglass feeling cold. Lincoln was fighting a war against slaveholders, Douglass complained in July 1861, yet he was doing so "without fighting slavery." The Confederates were "tearing up railways" and "building forts, guarding forts, fighting behind batteries," and all the while, their slaves were "busily at work with spade, shovel, plow and hoe." Slave labor was simultaneously aiding the insurrection and sustaining the rebel home front. "Why, in the name of all that is national," wondered Douglass, "does our Government allow its enemies this powerful advantage?"[4]

Lincoln had a different view. To Douglass's dismay, Lincoln was prepared to leave slavery alone if the rebels would only return to the fold. His one and only goal as commander in chief, Lincoln stressed, was to preserve the Union, not to fight a war to free the slaves. Just as bad, Lincoln seemed indifferent (or worse) to the idea of training, equipping, and making use of black troops, even in the Union's most desperate hour of need. "The government consents only that Negroes shall smell powder in the character of cooks and body servants in the army," Douglass complained.[5] He had a much better idea, and he urged the Lincoln administration to implement it at once: "Let the slaves and free colored people be called into service and formed into a liberating army, to march into the South and raise the banner of Emancipation."[6] But Lincoln was not ready to authorize anything like that—at least not yet.

In the 1850s, when the antislavery movement was first becoming a real force in national politics, Frederick Douglass had distinguished himself as the conscience of that movement. While others were advising half measures, mild manners, or compromises, Douglass could always be counted on to offer an unbending case for liberty. In the earth-shaking years between 1861 and 1865, he would play a similar role on behalf of the Union war effort. "No war but an Abolition war," Douglass maintained, aiming his words at the president, at members of Congress, and at the American people at large. "No peace but an Abolition peace."[7] It took time, and the final results did not always live up to the splendor of the original message, but Douglass's abolitionist vision, or at least a decent approximation of it, did take hold in the end.

"Abolition or Destruction"

As far as Frederick Douglass was concerned, the path to victory was clear. The Confederates are waging a "war for the destruction of liberty," he wrote in the summer of 1861. Let it be met "with war for the destruction of slavery."[8] The Lincoln administration, however, had other ideas.

Take the case of Union general John C. Frémont. On August 30, 1861, Frémont, the commander of the Department of the West (and the 1856 Republican candidate for president), declared martial law in Missouri, ordered the death penalty for pro-Southern guerrillas, and freed the slaves of every avowed Confederate in the state. In other words, he issued an emancipation proclamation.

Frémont's actions did not go down so well in Washington. Lincoln responded promptly with a letter countermanding the death penalty order ("allow no man to be shot under the proclamation without first having my approbation or consent") and urging, though not ordering, the general to switch his stance on slavery. Congress, Lincoln pointed out, had just passed a law allowing for the military confiscation of rebel property, including slaves, so long as that property was being used for explicit military purposes. Frémont, however, had gone further, also freeing those slaves who were not directly assisting rebel troops. That was simply too far for Lincoln. "Liberating slaves of traitorous owners," Lincoln wrote, "will alarm our Southern Union friends and turn them against us."[9] Lincoln was then desperately trying to keep the slaveholding border states, such as Kentucky and Maryland, loyal to the Union, and he feared that Frémont's broad emancipatory command would serve to drive them out.

But Frémont refused to act on Lincoln's request. He told the president that he would only modify his proclamation under orders. So, Lincoln ordered it. In a follow-up communication, the president instructed the general that his proclamation must be "so modified, held, and construed as to conform to, and not to transcend, the provisions on the same subject contained in the act of Congress entitled, 'An act to confiscate property used for insurrectionary purposes.'"[10]

Lincoln's reversal of Frémont's proclamation was widely criticized in antislavery circles. Unsurprisingly, Frederick Douglass led the charge. "The pusillanimous and pro-slavery interference of President Lincoln" will spell doom for the Union, Douglass declared.[11] "Many blunders have been committed by the Government at Washington during this war, but this, we think, is the hugest of them all."[12] Unburdening himself in a letter to Gerrit Smith, Douglass wrote that he was "bewildered by the spectacle of moral blindness, infatuation and helpless imbecility which the Government of Lincoln presents. Is there hope?"[13] Douglass feared that there was not.

But it was not all gloom and doom. At the same time that he was lambasting Lincoln's treatment of Frémont, Douglass was setting aside old differences with his former friend and mentor, William Lloyd Garrison. To be sure, Douglass had not forgotten about (nor fully forgiven) Garrison's various attempts to smear his name and reputation. But now, with the war at hand, Douglass felt as though he could afford to be a little generous. Plus, Garrison was plainly in need of a handout. As Douglass recognized, the bulk of Garrison's program—the pacifism, the nonvoting, the case for Northern secession—had been rendered worthless by the course of events. That left Garrison with little choice but to reach out in Douglass's direction and pivot toward Douglass's point of view. "A pleasing feature of the times is the readiness and heartiness with which all classes of abolitionists co-operate for the common cause," Douglass observed in March 1862. "Every man who is ready to work for the overthrow of slavery, whether . . . a Garrisonian or a Gerrit Smith man, black or white, is both clansman and kinsmen of ours. We form a common league against slavery."[14] Douglass, the onetime student, had now fully eclipsed his old teacher.

A month later, on April 16, Douglass received his best news yet since the fighting began. President Lincoln had signed a law that day, duly passed by both houses of Congress, abolishing slavery in Washington DC. For decades, this had been a goal of the abolitionist movement. In the 1830s, when John Quincy Adams took on the gag rule in the House of Representatives, he had done so on behalf of petitions to Congress praying for the abolition of slavery in the District of Columbia. Douglass himself once said that it was because of those petitions, and the roaring national debate they ignited, that he first learned "that there was a large and growing class of people in the north called abolitionists, who were moving for our freedom."[15] Now, almost a year to the day since the Civil War began, that freedom would become a reality for slaves living in the nation's capital.

"I trust I am not dreaming but the events taking place seem like a dream," Douglass wrote in celebration to Senator Charles Sumner of Massachusetts, one of the driving forces behind the success of the legislation in Congress. "Slavery is really dead in the District of Columbia. . . . I rejoice for my freed brothers, and Sir, I rejoice for you." Sumner, who had spent several years recovering from the terrible head injuries he sustained in 1856 at the hands of the cane-wielding South Carolinian Preston Brooks, had "lived," Douglass wrote, "to strike down in Washington, the power which lifted the bludgeon against your own free voice."[16]

It was a victory for Douglass's free voice too. Since his break with Garrison in 1851, Douglass had been a preeminent advocate of constitutional action against slavery. That action would now occur in the symbolic heart of the nation.

Unfortunately for Douglass, his feelings of elation would not last long. Once again, Lincoln was the source of his woes. On May 9, Union general David Hunter, commander of the Department of the South, issued an order declaring martial law in Georgia, Florida, and South Carolina. As part of that order, all persons in those states "heretofore held as slaves" were set free.[17] It was the Frémont scenario all over again. A general in the field had issued another emancipation proclamation. And just as he did before, Lincoln slapped the general down.

"Neither General Hunter, nor any other commander or person, has been authorized by the Government of the United States to make a proclamation declaring the slaves of any State free," Lincoln responded in a May 19 proclamation of his own. Hunter's order "is altogether void."[18]

This was almost more than Douglass could stomach. Why did the president reject the evidence that was plainly before him? Why did he refuse to fight the war in the one and only way in which it could be won? Speaking on July 4 in Yates County, New York, Douglass gave full vent to his mounting anger and frustration. Lincoln "was elected and inaugurated as the representative of the anti-slavery policy of the Republican Party." Yet how had he governed? How had he acquitted himself as commander in chief? "I do not hesitate to say, that whatever may have been his intentions, the action of President Lincoln has been calculated in a marked and decided way to shield and protect slavery from the very blows which its horrible crimes have loudly and persistently invited." Not only had Lincoln refused to wield the necessary powers that were at his disposal, Douglass complained, but he "repeatedly interfered with and arrested the anti-slavery policy of some of his most earnest and reliable generals." The president should have announced the freedom of every slave and welcomed them "into the lines of our army." Instead, he "submitted himself to the guidance of the half loyal slave states," meaning the border states, rather than listen to the steadfast voices of liberty emanating from the North.[19]

Make no mistake, Douglass concluded, Lincoln's hands-off policy toward slavery would inevitably fail; it would lose the war. As long as slavery was allowed to survive, it would remain "the great dominating interest" in the South, "overtopping all others" and forever corrupting the American body politic. "The only choice left to this nation," Douglass declared, "is abolition or destruction. You must abolish slavery or abandon the union."[20]

Douglass did not yet know it at the time, but Lincoln was quietly reaching the same conclusion.

"All the Laws but One"

Additional evidence of Frederick Douglass's enthusiasm for a vigorous war effort may be gleaned from his response to President Lincoln's wartime record on civil liberties. To put it mildly, complaints about executive overreach in this area dogged Lincoln throughout the conflict. Take the issue of habeas corpus, which is the venerable legal principle designed to prevent the government from indefinitely detaining those who are suspected—though not convicted—of illegal activity. When a judge issues a writ of habeas corpus, the government must either make its case or set the prisoner free.

There is one notable exception to that rule. According to Article I, Section 9 of the Constitution, "The Privilege of the Writ of Habeas Corpus shall not be suspended, unless when in Cases of Rebellion or Invasion the public Safety may require it." Article I, it is worth pausing here to note, is the part of the Constitution that spells out the powers of Congress. Yet on April 27, 1861, Lincoln, whose powers as president are spelled out in Article II, issued the following order to General Winfield Scott: "If at any point on or in the vicinity of any military line which shall be used between the city of Philadelphia and the city of Washington you find resistance which renders it necessary to suspend the writ of *habeas corpus* for the public safety, you personally, or through the officer in command at the point at which resistance occurs, are authorized to suspend that writ."[21]

Congress was not in session at that time and thus never authorized this order. Lincoln simply acted alone in the name of national security. As a wartime president who could practically smell the Confederate campfires burning across the Potomac River in Virginia, Lincoln needed to make safe the national capital. He also needed a well-trained army on the march. When it came down to it, what he needed was a steady supply of troops from the North. And the quickest way for those troops to get to Washington was to travel by rail, a journey that took them through the slaveholding (though nonsecessionist) border state of Maryland. But this journey posed some problems. There was the risk of guerrilla attacks on troop transports. There was also the risk of guerrilla sabotage of both the railroads and the communication lines. And then there was Baltimore, a city where Confederate sympathies ran high. Troops arriving from the North had to disembark in one part of that city and then walk several blocks across town in order to board their southbound connecting trains to Washington. There had already been some incidents of mob violence along that particular part of the route.

Thus the presidential suspension of habeas corpus. Lock up the troublemakers, Lincoln told General Scott, and get me those troops. On May 25 the order was put into effect when a man named John Merryman, who had been organizing Confederate recruits in Baltimore, was arrested by Union forces and locked up at nearby Fort McHenry. Later that same day, Merryman's lawyer filed a petition for a writ of habeas corpus at the U.S. District Court for the District of Maryland. That petition landed on the desk of none other than Chief Justice Roger Taney.

In addition to his duties at the Supreme Court, Taney, like every other justice at that time in the court's history, also heard a certain number of cases each year as a federal circuit court judge. It was in that capacity that Taney, the author of *Dred Scott*, entered the fray over Lincoln's suspension of habeas corpus.

A series of courtroom confrontations promptly followed. On May 26 Taney signed the writ, ordering General George Cadwalader, the commander of Fort McHenry, to appear before the circuit court, bringing John Merryman in tow. On May 27 one of General Cadwalader's officers showed up to court instead, without Merryman. That officer proceeded to tell Taney that the general was acting on orders from the president and would require additional orders from that source before proceeding any further in regards to the prisoner. The federal court order, in short, would not be obeyed.

Taney was furious. "General Cadwalader was commanded to produce the body of Mr. Merryman before me this morning, that the case might be heard, and the petitioner either be remanded to custody, or set at liberty, if held on insufficient grounds," Taney declared, "but he has acted in disobedience to the writ."[22] On May 28, in an opinion for the circuit court, Taney directed his ire even further up the chain of military command. "I had supposed it to be one of those points of constitutional law upon which there was no difference of opinion, and that it was admitted on all hands," Taney wrote, "that the privilege of the writ of habeas corpus could not be suspended, except by act of Congress."[23] Yet here was the president of the United States openly disregarding the constitutional separation of powers.

If the government has evidence against Merryman, Taney maintained, that evidence should be turned over to the district attorney so that proper charges may be filed and Merryman may be arrested and prosecuted in civilian court. That is what due process of law requires in such cases. But instead of doing that, Taney wrote, the president has not only defied a federal court order, but he "has, by force of arms, thrust aside the judicial authorities and . . . substituted a military government, to be administered and executed by military officers."[24]

To avoid any misunderstanding of the court's ruling, Taney then added that he was ordering the circuit court clerk "to transmit a copy" of his opinion, "under seal, to the President of the United States. It will then remain for that high officer, in fulfillment of his constitutional obligation to 'take care that the laws be faithfully executed,' to determine what measures he will take to cause the civil process of the United States to be respected, and enforced."[25]

Taney's judgment did not produce the desired effect. In the words of historian Bruce Catton, "Lincoln controlled the soldiers and Taney did not, and the arrest stuck."[26]

Lincoln did finally respond to Taney's ruling in a message that he sent to a special session of Congress on July 4, 1861. "The attention of the country has been called to the proposition that one who has sworn to 'take care that the laws be faithfully executed' should not himself violate them," Lincoln observed. But consider the context in which the executive action was undertaken. The suspension of habeas corpus occurred at a point in time when "the whole of the laws which were required to be faithfully executed were being resisted" by the secessionist states. Must those laws, Lincoln asked, "be allowed to finally fail of execution" in order that the right of habeas corpus, which "relieves more of the guilty than the innocent," be enforced? "To state the question more directly, are all the laws but one to go unexecuted, and the government itself go to pieces lest that one be

violated?" What if "disregarding the single law would tend to preserve" the Union?[27] Didn't the president therefore have a sworn duty
to disregard that single law?

This was about as close as Lincoln would come to acknowledging
that he had in fact violated the Constitution in the name of saving
it. Then, having come so close to acknowledgment, Lincoln swiftly
changed course, arguing that his actions had been perfectly lawful
all along. Habeas corpus may be suspended "in case of rebellion or
invasion," Lincoln noted. Because "it was decided that we have a
case of rebellion," the commander in chief was thus fully authorized
to act. "As the provision [for suspending the writ of habeas corpus]
was plainly made for a dangerous emergency," Lincoln asserted, "it
cannot be believed the framers of the instrument intended that in
every case the danger should run its course until Congress could
be called together."[28]

Constitutional scholars have been arguing about the legality of
Lincoln's actions ever since. For his part, Frederick Douglass pro-
fessed himself fully satisfied with the president's justifications. "As
the war progresses," Douglass wrote in 1862, "the great writ of habeas
corpus is suspended from necessity, liberty of speech and of the
press have ceased to exist." Douglass was referring to the fact that
federal authorities had also imprisoned a number of antiwar edi-
tors in the North. For example, James McMaster, the editor of New
York's *Freeman's Journal*, was locked away for eleven weeks in Fort
Lafayette, on the order of the secretary of state, before finally being
set free. He was never brought to trial. "One stroke of the pen" by
Lincoln "sends any citizen to prison, as in England, three centuries
ago, British subjects were sent to the Tower of London," Douglass
wrote. "I speak this not in complaint," he added. "I admit the necessity, while I lament it."[29]

Such was the extent of Frederick Douglass's handwringing over
the Lincoln administration's wartime crackdown on civil liberties.

"Forever Free"

In his May 1862 order voiding General Hunter's emancipation policy
for Georgia, Florida, and South Carolina, Abraham Lincoln wrote

that if anybody was going to liberate slaves as a military necessity, it would be the commander in chief, not some general acting on his own initiative. These "are questions, which, under my responsibility, I reserve to myself."[30] Though little noticed at the time, especially by critics such as Frederick Douglass, that statement by Lincoln was a preview of things to come.

The notion that slavery might be lawfully abolished through an exercise of the war powers long predated Lincoln's days in the White House. Indeed, none other than John Quincy Adams, the former president turned member of Congress, raised that very notion during his showdown in the late 1830s over the gagging of abolitionist petitions in the House of Representatives. Throughout that debate, as we have seen, the proslavery contingent insisted that the Constitution gave the federal government no power whatsoever over slavery in those places in which the institution already existed.

Do not be so sure about that, replied the wily congressman from Massachusetts. What happens if war breaks out on U.S. soil? "Do you suppose that your Congress will have no constitutional authority to interfere with the institution of slavery in any way" under that scenario? If such a war comes, Adams argued, the federal government "must and will interfere" with slavery, "perhaps to sustain it by war; perhaps to abolish it by treaties of peace." Either way, the "local" institution will undoubtedly come under the purview of the national authorities. "From the instant that your slaveholding States become the theatre of war, civil, servile, or foreign," Adams observed, "from that instant the war powers of Congress extend to interference with the institution of slavery in every way by which it can be interfered with."[31]

By the summer of 1862, Lincoln had decided that interfering with slavery was precisely what he needed to do if the Northern cause was going to prevail. "My paramount objective in this struggle is to save the Union," Lincoln wrote to Horace Greeley, the editor of the *New York Tribune*, on August 22. "If I could save the Union without freeing any slave, I would do it; and if I could save it by freeing all the slaves, I would do it; and if I could save it by freeing some and leaving others alone, I would also do that."[32] What Lincoln did not tell Greeley was that he had already decided to pursue the third of those three courses of action.

On July 22 Lincoln gathered his cabinet and told them that he held in his hand a preliminary order freeing every slave in rebel territory. What General Hunter had recently sought to do in just three states, Lincoln was now prepared to do throughout the entire Confederacy.

The cabinet was largely receptive to the idea, though Secretary of State William Seward did offer one piece of strategic advice. Postpone the announcement "until you can give it to the country supported by military success," Seward recommended. The Union army had just suffered a string of defeats, and to free the slaves now might look like "the last measure of an exhausted government, a cry for help."[33] Lincoln would heed this counsel. The Emancipation Proclamation was placed on the shelf, awaiting military victory.

Victory arrived on September 17. Two weeks earlier, Confederate general Robert E. Lee had invaded the North, marching his formidable Army of Northern Virginia across the Potomac River into Maryland. "Destroy the rebel army if possible," Lincoln telegrammed Union major general George B. McClellan, who was now compelled to reorient his own Army of the Potomac in order to meet the invading Southern foe.[34] These two mighty forces eventually collided in the sleepy town of Sharpsburg, Maryland, where a winding local waterway, known as the Antietam Creek, gave the battle its now storied name.

What followed was the single bloodiest day of fighting of the entire Civil War, a twelve-hour conflagration that left some twenty-three thousand men killed, wounded, or missing. "The ground was so thickly carpeted with dead men," the historian Shelby Foote has written, "that one witness claimed you could walk in any direction across it and never touch the ground."[35] Among the casualties that day was twenty-one-year-old Oliver Wendell Holmes Jr., a captain in the Twentieth Massachusetts Regiment and future associate justice of the U.S. Supreme Court. He was shot through the neck and left for dead. "Some sharp burning pain in left shoulder," Holmes wrote home to his mother a day later, "yet it don't seem to have smashed my spine or I suppose I should be dead or paralyzed or something."[36]

The Army of the Potomac ultimately emerged the winner, having penetrated the Confederate center and forced a retreat. Yet it was not the overwhelming triumph that had been hoped for. Despite Lincoln's instruction to "destroy the rebel army if possible," McClellan failed to throw his superior numbers at Lee's backtracking forces. The Army of Northern Virginia went home licking its wounds, but it would live to fight another day.

Still, this strategic victory would serve Lincoln's purposes. On September 22 he assembled his cabinet and returned again to the topic of emancipation. Secretary of the Treasury Salmon P. Chase, the veteran antislavery lawyer whom Lincoln would later name to the Supreme Court, recorded the scene in his diary. "I think the time has now come," Lincoln said. "The action of the army against the rebels has not quite been what I should have liked best, but they have been driven out of Maryland, and Pennsylvania is no longer in danger of invasion."[37] Lincoln informed the cabinet that he would now release what he called the preliminary Emancipation Proclamation.

It was preliminary because it did not go into effect immediately. "On the first day of January, in the year of our Lord, one thousand eight hundred and sixty-three," the document declared, "all persons held as slaves within any State the people whereof shall then be in rebellion against the United States, shall be then, thenceforward, and forever free."[38]

Frederick Douglass was jubilant at the news. "We shout for joy that we live to record this righteous decree," he cheered.[39] Of course, the first of January was still more than three months away. Would the president change his mind in the interim? Would the South surrender before the order went into effect, thereby preserving the prewar status quo? Many an abolitionist would pass a sleepless night during that long interval.

For Douglass, the last few hours of waiting may have been the hardest of all. On New Year's Eve, he gathered with thousands of others at Boston's Tremont Temple, waiting on pins and needles for the official order of emancipation to come in over the wires. "I shall never forget that memorable night," he later recalled. "Nor shall I ever forget the outburst of joy and thanksgiving that rent the air when the lightening brought to us the emancipation proclamation."[40] In that electric moment, Douglass could practically taste victory.

In the sober light of morning, the proclamation would appear somewhat less dramatic. It did nothing, after all, for those slaves who resided in the border states, since "the people whereof" were not "in rebellion" and thus their states were not covered by the decree. Douglass surely felt the sting when he considered that Maryland, the state where he had spent the first twenty years of his life trapped in bondage, and where members of his own family still languished in chains, was left untouched by the Emancipation Proclamation. Was this really victory?

It was. Looking back a few years later, Douglass explained that he "took the proclamation, first and last, for a little more than it purported." Yes, the document had its shortcomings. But its "moral power would extend much further" than its careful, legalistic text. "Its meaning to me was the entire abolition of slavery, wherever the evil could be reached by the Federal arm."[41] Once set in motion by the Emancipation Proclamation, Douglass believed, the logic of abolitionism could not be contained by any such geographic restrictions.

"I Urge You to Fly to Arms"

Frederick Douglass pursued twin goals throughout the Civil War. One involved convincing the federal government to adopt an abolitionist policy; the other involved persuading that same government to equip black troops and send them into battle against the South's proslavery regime. "From the first," he later explained in *Life and Times of Frederick Douglass*, the third and final autobiography that he would write, "I reproached the North that they fought the rebels with only one hand, when they might strike effectually with two—that they fought with their soft white hand, while they kept their black iron hand chained and helpless behind them."[42] In the early months of 1863, the state of Massachusetts gave Douglass the chance to help unshackle that black iron hand.

The governor of Massachusetts at that time was a man named John A. Andrew. He was an opponent of slavery and, like Douglass, wanted to see black troops dressed in Union blue. After repeatedly lobbying the Lincoln administration to that end, the governor finally got his wish. On January 26, 1863, the War Department, with the winds of change inaugurated by the Emancipation Proclamation blowing at its back, authorized Andrew to raise "such corps of infantry for the volunteer military service as he may find convenient," including "persons of African descent, organized into special corps."[43]

The governor got to work. On January 30 he wrote a letter to the prominent Boston lawyer and abolitionist Francis G. Shaw, describing his vision of a vanguard force that "may be a model for all future colored regiments." Its officers should be "young men of military experience," Andrew wrote, "of firm antislavery principles, ambitious, superior to a vulgar contempt for color, and having faith in the capacity of colored men for military service."[44] In fact, Andrew admitted, he already had one such young man in mind: Shaw's twenty-five-year-old son, Robert Gould Shaw, who was then serving as a captain in the Second Massachusetts Infantry. Talk to your boy, the governor urged, and pass along my offer of a formal commission as colonel of this new regiment. The father did as Andrew requested, and the son took the job.

In the meantime, the governor put together a committee charged with supervising the overall recruitment of black troops for the state. Among its members was his old friend George L. Stearns, a Republican stalwart and longtime antislavery activist. Stearns recognized that the Bay State, with its relatively small black population, might not yield forth a sufficient number of enlisted men. So on February 23, Stearns hit the road for New York. Stopping in Rochester, he paid a visit to Frederick Douglass, whom he hoped to sign on as a recruiting agent. Douglass did not need to be asked twice. A few days later, Douglass produced one of his most memorable statements on the war effort, a stirring broadside titled "Men of Color, to Arms!"

From the moment that Fort Sumter was attacked, Douglass wrote, he had pushed the federal government to employ black troops. "With every reverse to the national arms, with every exulting shout of victory raised by the slaveholding rebels," he had advised this course of action.[45] Who better to fight a war against a slaveholding regime than the very people it desired to enslave? True, Douglass conceded, the Lincoln administration had not heeded this wise advice until quite recently. The Union leadership had dragged its feet while the armies of the Confederacy gained ground. But such complaints, valid as they were, must wait. "When the war is over," Douglass wrote, "and the black man's rights are secured, as they will be, history with an impartial hand will dispose of that and sundry other questions."[46] Now, he stressed, was the time to fight. "I wish I could tell you that the State of New York calls you to this high honor," Douglass added. But "we can get at the throat of treason and slavery through the State of Massachusetts," and that was more than sufficient for the crucial task at hand. "The case is before you," Douglass declared. "I urge you to fly to arms."[47]

With his argument spelled out in print, Douglass set about putting his oratorical talents to use as well. "I have visited Buffalo and obtained seven good men," he wrote in a March 6 letter to Gerrit Smith. "I spoke here [in Rochester] last night and got thirteen. I shall visit Auburn, Syracuse, Ithaca, Troy and Albany and other places in the State till I get one hundred men." With a touch of pride, he informed Smith that his call to arms "was published in all the papers here, and is having a good effect." He also shared another reason why he was well pleased with his recruiting work so far: "Charley my youngest was the first to put his name down as one of the company."[48] His oldest son, Lewis, enlisted too.

They would join the ranks of the Fifty-Fourth Massachusetts Volunteer Infantry, an outfit destined to enter the annals of American military history. Just as Governor Andrew intended, the Fifty-Fourth would be the North's showpiece all-black regiment. Through valor and force of arms, the hundreds of free black men who joined up would stake their claim to the rights and privileges of U.S. citizenship. They would take abolitionist principles and put them into action. "This is our golden opportunity," Douglass wrote in his call to arms. "Let us accept it, and forever wipe out the dark reproaches unsparingly hurled against us by our enemies."[49]

The process was not always an easy one. As the men trained at Camp Readville, located a few miles outside of downtown Boston, they were subjected to many racist taunts and objections. Some whites asserted that blacks lacked the courage to fight. Others claimed that they would never adhere to military discipline. "The mustering-officer, who was here to-day, is a Virginian, and has always thought it was a great joke to try and make soldiers" out of blacks, Colonel Shaw wrote home to his father on March 6. But even that mustering officer, hardened old bigot that he was, had to accept the evidence that came before him. "He told me to-day, that he had never mustered in so fine a set of men [as the Fifty-Fourth], though about twenty thousand had passed through his hands since September last," Robert Gould Shaw proudly informed his father. "The sceptics need only come out here now, to be converted."[50] Two months later, when the Fifty-Fourth Massachusetts finally saw action in South Carolina, the skeptics would be silenced for good.

The order to ship out arrived on May 18. The Fifty-Fourth was told to report to General David Hunter, who was then conducting operations along the South Carolina coast. Ten days later, the regiment was packed, organized, and ready to go. Winding its way through the streets of Boston, the Fifty-Fourth marched proudly to Battery Wharf, where a steamer awaited. "Vast crowds lined the streets where the regiment was to pass," one journalist reported, "and the Common was crowded with an immense number of people such as only the Fourth of July or some rare event causes to assemble."[51] Marching along Essex Street, the Fifty-Fourth passed in front of the home of the abolitionist Wendell Phillips. According to one veteran's account, William Lloyd Garrison could be seen standing on Phillips's balcony. A few years earlier, Garrison had been an outspoken advocate of "non-resistance," rejecting the use of "all carnal weapons for deliverance from bondage."[52] His newspaper, the Liberator, had even upbraided Reverend Henry Highland Garnet for speaking out in support of slave revolts. But now, with hundreds of black troops filing past him, including Frederick Douglass's son Lewis, who carried the rank of sergeant major, Garrison seemed to view the matter in a somewhat different light. Garrison stood there, the witness said, with "his hand resting on the head of a bust of John Brown."[53]

"That Musket Means Liberty"

With the Fifty-Fourth Massachusetts headed off to war, Frederick Douglass agreed to take on a few additional recruiting duties. July 6, for example, found him in Philadelphia, Pennsylvania, speaking to a mass meeting organized by George Stearns, who was now assisting the federal government in enrolling black troops in other parts of the country. Philadelphia had recently received permission from the War Department to raise an all-black division, and Stearns had brought Douglass down to deliver the principal recruiting pitch to potential enlistees.

Douglass told the crowd to consider the big picture. Two very different governments were battling for dominance, he said, and the question for black Americans was simple, "Which is for us, and which against us?" The "Jefferson Davis government holds out to us nothing but fetters, chains, auction blocks, bludgeons, branding-irons, and eternal slavery and degradation."[54] That government was the sworn enemy of each and every black person and was to be handled as such. But what about the government of Lincoln? Was it any better? Yes, it was, Douglass declared, particularly when judged in the light of its course of action. The government of Lincoln had now abolished slavery in the District of Columbia. It had forbidden slavery in the federal territories. It had proclaimed emancipation throughout each and every rebel state. What is more, "abolish slavery tomorrow, and not a sentence or syllable of the Constitution need be altered. It was purposely so framed as to give no claim, no sanction to the claim, of property in man."[55] That was the government worth fighting for.

But you must also fight for yourselves, he told the crowd. You must fight for your dignity, for your fundamental rights as citizens. "Slavery can be abolished by white men," he pointed out, "but liberty so won for the black man, while it may leave him an object of pity, can never make him an object of respect."[56]

"Remember," Douglass told the audience in conclusion, "that the musket—the United States musket with its bayonet of steel—is better than all mere parchment guarantees of liberty. In your hands that musket means liberty." And remember something else. If anyone seeks to deprive you of that liberty, you and "your brethren are safe while you have a Constitution which proclaims your right to keep and bear arms."[57]

"We Did Our Duty as Men"

The Fifty-Fourth Massachusetts Volunteer Infantry got its first taste of battle in the early morning hours of July 16, 1863. A week earlier, the regiment had received orders to link up with Brigadier General Alfred Terry, whose division was slated to take part in the latest phase of the large, ongoing battle for control of Charleston, South Carolina. The overall Union strategy went like this: The mouth of Charleston harbor is formed by two islands, Sullivan's Island to the north and Morris Island to the south. Between them, sitting on a much smaller man-made island in the middle of the harbor, is Fort Sumter. To gain control of the city, the Union general Quincy Gillmore, the commander of the Department of the South, planned to seize Morris Island; use it as a position from which to batter and neutralize Fort Sumter; and then, as a prelude to the final invasion, send in naval forces to clear the inner harbor and its channels.

General Terry's division of four thousand was assigned a diversionary role. Instead of joining the main attack on Morris Island, Terry's forces were to make a demonstration on James Island, which sits to the northwest of Morris and is located much closer to the city. The Fifty-Fourth Massachusetts was placed on the extreme right of Terry's line.

The James Island diversion worked even better than expected. The Confederate general P. G. T. Beauregard, concerned that the assault on Charleston might actually be coming his way via James Island, sent a force of six hundred to attack Terry's right. When those rebels struck at dawn on July 16, they came crashing into the Fifty-Fourth Massachusetts. Had the untested Northern regiment broken apart under the sudden pressure, the entire Union line on James Island might have followed suit. But the men held together, and the Confederate attack soon sputtered and died. Under fire for the first time, the Fifty-Fourth performed wonderfully. "It is not for us to blow our horn," one veteran later wrote. "But when a regiment of white men gave us three cheers as we were passing them [after the fight], it shows that we did our duty as men."[58]

Meanwhile, on Morris Island, the principal Union attack had reached a stalemate. At the northern end of the island, taking up its entire width, was a massive Confederate earthworks known as Fort Wagner. After a week of fighting, the Union forces controlled the bulk of the island, but Wagner remained firmly in the hands of the Confederates. On July 11, after a lengthy bombardment, the Union launched a frontal assault on the fortress, but it failed to dislodge the garrison inside. Undeterred, General Gillmore was now ready to try again. "With the combined fire of the land batteries and gunboats," Gillmore later wrote in his official report, he intended "to dismount the principal guns of the work [Fort Wagner], and either drive the enemy from it or open the way to a successful assault."[59]

So stood the plan as of July 16.

"The Most Desperate Charge of the War"

If you have seen the 1989 Hollywood film *Glory*, which depicts the exploits of the Fifty-Fourth Massachusetts Volunteer Infantry, starring Mathew Broderick as Colonel Robert Gould Shaw and Denzel Washington as a private named Silas Trip, you probably remember the scene at the campfire. It is the night before the big battle. The Fifty-Fourth are set to lead the charge against Fort Wagner the next day, and the men get to enjoy one last moment of uneasy calm before the storm. They pray, sing songs, and contemplate the larger meaning of what they are about to do.

It is a terrific scene. Unfortunately, it bears little resemblance to reality. The Fifty-Fourth did not get to enjoy a final night of peaceful reflection before charging Fort Wagner, because the regiment only received the assignment about two hours before the attack was launched. And the men were anything but rested. In fact, they had just spent the better part of two days on the move, with no rations, little water, and even less sleep.

After fending off the Confederate attack in the early hours of July 16, the Fifty-Fourth joined the rest of Terry's division in vacating James Island. It was a slow, laborious process. The men would march, wait around for transport, crowd into steamers, and then march again. Eventually, around 5:00 p.m. on July 18, they arrived, footsore and hungry, at the Union position on Morris Island. It was then that Colonel Shaw was presented with the opportunity for the Fifty-Fourth to lead the frontal assault on Fort Wagner, which was scheduled to kick off around 7:00. "Shaw's face brightened," one of his officers later wrote, and he accepted the honor.[60] The time had come for the North's vanguard black regiment to demonstrate what it could do.

The Fifty-Fourth Massachusetts confronted a daunting sight as it took its place at the tip of the spear. Fort Wagner loomed about a thousand yards ahead. To get there, the men had to march along a strip of land that was, at the most, a few hundred yards wide. On their immediate right was the Atlantic Ocean, its shoreline running parallel to their path. Because the attack was set for sundown, which was just a few hours after high tide that day, those lined up on the far right would be forced, in the words of one veteran, "to march in water up to their knees, at each incoming of the sea."[61] On the left side of the path was a marsh, formed by the nearby Vincent's Creek. Closer to the fort, about 150 yards out from its walls, the terrain changed, with the marsh jutting eastward. This narrowed the strip of walkable land significantly, reducing it down to a width of about twenty-five yards during high tide. This meant that the men, as they closed in on their target, would have to start bunching up, everybody pushing in toward the center as they raced forward. That was bad enough. To make matters worse, the eastward jut of the marsh also forced the attackers to turn slightly leftward as they made their final rush at the walls. This created what military strategists call an enfilade. In effect, the fort's defenders would now be in a position to fire directly into and along the exposed right flank of the Union attack.

And all of that assumed that everything went according to plan— which it did not. "Up to this period, our actual knowledge of the strength of the enemy's defenses on the north end of Morris Island was quite meager," General Gillmore later acknowledged in his official report. Gillmore's entire strategy rested on the notion that the

Union's extensive bombardment of the fortress would either kill, injure, or otherwise dislodge most of the garrison inside, thereby paving the way for a successful frontal assault while at the same time reducing the obvious risk of enfilading fire. But the bombardment did not accomplish anything of the sort. Regrettably, as Gillmore observed in his report, "the truly formidable character of Fort Wagner and the great strength and capacity of its bomb-proof shelter were very much underestimated."[62]

Gillmore's counterpart, P. G. T. Beauregard, could have told him as much, had the Southern general been inclined to share such valuable intelligence, which he most certainly was not. "Another attack is expected soon," Beauregard wired to his superiors in Richmond, Virginia, on the morning of July 16. "Am preparing for it." Twelve hours later he sent off another communication. "Enemy is massing his troops on Morris Island, evidently for another attack on Battery Wagner," Beauregard reported. "Their monitors, gunboats, and mortar-boats keep up an almost constant fire all day on that work, with little damage to it and few casualties."[63] Beauregard knew what was coming and was ready to meet it. Indeed, as the historian Dudley Taylor Cornish has observed, "there was no possibility of surprise: preparations for the assault, every movement of the Union troops, were observed from Wagner and other Confederate works in the vicinity."[64] As the men of the Fifty-Fourth assembled in marching order on the beach, Fort Wagner sat silently in waiting, ready to spring like a trap.

At 7:45 p.m. Colonel Shaw gave the order to step off. "Move in quick time until within a hundred yards of the fort," Shaw told his men. "Then double quick and charge! Forward!"[65]

Off they went, with flags waving and bayonets glinting in whatever last rays of sunlight still remained. They marched for hundreds of yards, unmolested. But the flaws in the Union plan soon became evident. "When we arrived within a short distance of the works," reported Lieutenant James Grace of the Fifty-Fourth, "the Rebels opened up on us with grape and cannister accompanied with a thousand muskets, mowing our men down by the hundreds."[66] Fort Wagner suddenly became "a mound of fire," recalled Captain Luis

F. Emilio. "A sheet of flame, followed by a running fire, like electric sparks, swept along the parapet."[67] Sergeant Major Lewis Douglass, the oldest son of the great abolitionist, would report that "men fell all around me."[68] It was, he later told his parents, "the most desperate charge of the war."[69]

The attackers reeled at the impact of the Confederate blast, staggered, and then surged forward yet again, only to meet the same deadly welcome. "Such a tremendous fire right in our faces caused us to fall back," reported one veteran.[70] Remarkably, those who were not killed outright at that point kept going and succeeded not only in reaching the fortress but in scaling its walls, some as high as thirty feet, and fighting its defenders at their own guns. "We went at it," recalled Corporal James Gooding. "We met the foe on the parapet of Wagner with the bayonet."[71] Somewhere amid that bloody hand-to-hand combat, with blades slashing and guns firing, Sergeant Major Douglass suffered a nasty groin wound and had the sheath of his sword blown off from his hip. Had that shot landed just a few inches in another direction, it easily could have killed him. "How I got out of that fight alive," he later wrote to his fiancée, Amelia Loguen, "I cannot tell."[72]

The fighting kept on like that, on and around the fortress walls for nearly an hour. At one point, the U.S. flag was even seen waving from the crest of the parapet. But the Fifty-Fourth, or what was left of it, simply could not hold the position. The men were outnumbered on those walls, and outgunned. Additional regiments had followed them in, but there was never sufficient support to hold the ground that was gained. At last, the surviving attackers fell back in retreat. "Mortal men could not stand such a fire," declared Corporal Gooding, who was plainly shocked that he had somehow managed to survive the inferno.[73]

It was late into the night when the shooting finally stopped for good. At 3:40 a.m. General Beauregard sent word of victory to Richmond. "After furious bombardment—eleven hours—from ships and shore, throwing many thousand shots and shells, enemy assaulted Battery Wagner desperately and repeatedly, beginning at dark. Our people fought worthily," he declared, "and repulsed attacks with great slaughter."[74]

The Union's losses that night would prove staggering. Of the six hundred members of the Fifty-Fourth Massachusetts Volunteer Infantry who led the charge against Fort Wagner, for instance, nearly half were killed, wounded, or captured. Among those casualties were a number of ranking officers, including the regiment's young commander, Colonel Robert Gould Shaw, who was shot through the heart on the parapet. His body would later be thrown in a ditch by the Confederates and buried with his fallen troops.

"The Heaviest Blow"

Military historians generally rank the month of July 1863 as one of the turning points of the Civil War. It was on July 3, for example, that Robert E. Lee's second invasion of the North was beaten back in Gettysburg, Pennsylvania. After that famous defeat, the Army of Northern Virginia would never again threaten the Union on Northern soil. Meanwhile, one day later and some seven hundred miles away to the west, Ulysses S. Grant brought his months-long siege of Vicksburg, Mississippi, to a successful close. Never again would the rebels command the Mississippi River from that city's imposing bluffs. With the loss of that strategic stronghold, the days of the Confederacy were numbered.

The Battle of Fort Wagner, fought on July 18, was a turning point, too, though of a different sort. Unlike Gettysburg and Vicksburg, Fort Wagner was not a Union victory. Indeed, it was a crushing Union defeat. Yet at the same time, it was a powerful moral victory for the men of the Fifty-Fourth Massachusetts Volunteer Infantry and all that they represented. As Sergeant Major Lewis Douglass wrote to his fiancée, in a letter sent two days after the bloodletting on Morris Island, "Remember if I die I die in a good cause."[75] His regiment's brave, doomed charge would dispel forever any lingering racist doubts about the courage and spirit of black troops.

The Battle of Fort Wagner also helped transform Union policy. "I desire that a renewed and vigorous effort be made to raise colored forces along the shores of the Mississippi," Lincoln wrote to Secretary of War Edward Stanton on July 21.[76] By the war's end, there would be over six hundred black regiments fighting for the national flag. On July 30 Lincoln took another fateful step. He finally agreed to punish the Confederates for their systematic mistreatment of captured black troops, whom they commonly sold off into slavery. "For every soldier of the United States killed in violation of the laws of war, a Rebel soldier shall be executed," Lincoln ordered, "and for every one enslaved by the enemy or sold into slavery, a Rebel soldier shall be placed at hard labor on the public works, and continue at such labor until the other shall be released and receive the same treatment due a prisoner of war."[77] The U.S. government still had a long way to go before it would treat its black soldiers on a fully equal basis with its white ones, but it was getting there.

A few weeks later, in an open letter dated August 26, Lincoln reflected on just how far the country had come since the volatile days following the 1861 attack on Fort Sumter. "Peace does not appear so distant as it did," he wrote.[78] And when that peace does finally come, "there will be some black men who can remember that with silent tongue, and clenched teeth, and steady eye, and well-poised bayonet, they have helped mankind on to this great consummation, while I fear there will be some white ones unable to forget that with malignant heart and deceitful speech they strove to hinder it."[79]

Lincoln also directed a few choice remarks at his critics. Let me "be plain," he wrote. "You dislike the emancipation proclamation, and perhaps would have it retracted. You say it is unconstitutional. I think differently." The Constitution, Lincoln argued, places "the law of war in time of war" in the hands of the federal government.[80] That is the legality of emancipation. As for its practicality, just look to the battlefield. "You say you will not fight to free negroes," Lincoln observed, a comment aimed at both Northern Democrats and moderate Republicans. "Some of them seem willing to fight for you."[81]

Two years earlier, when the conflict between the Union and the Confederacy was still in its infancy, Frederick Douglass had insisted that "war for the destruction of liberty must be met with war for the destruction of slavery."[82] By the summer of 1863, the contest was finally shaping up to be just that.

Lincoln had another practical point to make that August day. "Some of the commanders of our armies in the field," he wrote, "who have given us our most important successes, believe that the emancipation policy and the use of colored troops constitute the heaviest blow yet dealt to the rebellion."[83] Lincoln was referring to Grant, the hero of Vicksburg and, two years down the line, the vanquisher of Robert E. Lee. Grant was no radical abolitionist in those days. In fact, he had married into a family of slaveholders. But he did have a firm grasp on the mathematics of war. Writing to Lincoln on August 23, a little over a month after the men of the Fifty-Fourth Massachusetts had stormed Fort Wagner, Grant informed the president that he had "given the subject of arming the negro my hearty support." Black troops will make "a powerful ally," Grant wrote. "This, with the emancipation of the negro, is the heaviest blow yet given the Confederacy."[84]

Frederick Douglass could not have said it any better himself.

5

"One Nation, One Country, One Citizenship"

On May 10, 1865, William Lloyd Garrison addressed the thirty-second annual meeting of the American Anti-Slavery Society in New York City. It was a heady and momentous occasion. A little over a month before, at Appomattox Courthouse, Virginia, the Confederate general Robert E. Lee had surrendered to Ulysses S. Grant, the commanding general of the Union army. Meanwhile, that very morning, Jefferson Davis, the once powerful president of the Confederate States of America, had been captured by Union forces after several weeks in hiding and on the run. The Civil War was over at last.

So, too, was slavery. What had begun two years earlier with the Emancipation Proclamation was now culminating with the ratification of the Thirteenth Amendment to the U.S. Constitution. Passed by Congress on January 31 and currently winding its way through the states, where it would be officially ratified by the end of the year, the amendment declared, "Neither slavery nor involuntary servitude, except as a punishment for crime whereof the party shall have been duly convicted, shall exist within the United States, or any place subject to their jurisdiction." The word *slavery* would thus appear for the first and last time in the text of the Constitution, placed there for the express purpose of eliminating the institution once and for all.

"Slavery is abolished in this country; abolished constitutionally; abolished by a decree of this nation, never, never to be reversed,"

Garrison told his fellow abolitionists. He was beyond overjoyed. The work of the American Anti-Slavery Society, a group that Garrison had first helped to organize way back in 1833, was now complete. "This Society has essentially consummated its mission," Garrison declared. "Nothing is more clear in my own mind, nothing has been more clear, than that this is the fitting time to dissolve our organization." After all, Garrison observed, "slavery is in its grave, and there is no power in this nation that can ever bring it back."[1]

Frederick Douglass was not so sure about that. Yes, the enemy was defeated, Douglass told the same audience, speaking shortly after Garrison. But other dangers still lurked. Even with the Thirteenth Amendment in place, "the South, by unfriendly legislation, could make our liberty, under that provision, a delusion, a mockery, and a snare," Douglass observed. "What advantage is a provision like this Amendment to the black man, if the Legislature of any State can to-morrow declare that no black man's testimony shall be received in a court of law?"[2] As Douglass well understood, the formal end of slavery—as vital, triumphant, and long overdue as it was—did not necessarily mean the end of racist government abuse. So long as "the Black man can be denied a vote" and so long as "the Legislatures of the South can take from him the right to keep and bear arms," Douglass maintained, "the work of the Abolitionists is not finished."[3]

Douglass was right to be wary. In the aftermath of the Civil War, state and local governments throughout the South initiated a wave of new attacks on the constitutional freedoms of black Americans and their white Unionist allies. Most notably, through the tangled web of laws, regulations, and ordinances known as the Black Codes, these governments menaced the freedmen and freedwomen on virtually every front, targeting their rights to vote, assemble, speak freely, receive due process, travel, enjoy public accommodations, make contracts, own property, earn a living, and much else besides. In Florida, for instance, the legislative committee tasked with preparing that state's Black Code described its objective as "the protection of our wives and children from threatened danger."[4] That same committee also praised slavery for "constituting the happiest and best-provided-for laboring population of the world."[5]

To make matters worse, the U.S. Supreme Court effectively rubber-stamped this dire state of affairs. Beginning in the 1870s (and continuing into the twentieth century), the court largely refused to offer any meaningful judicial protection for civil rights and other fundamental liberties, including those liberties listed in the Bill of Rights. At the same time, the court severely diminished the scope of the Fourteenth Amendment, which was ratified in 1868 to protect both rights and equality against state infringement, and then mostly declined to enforce the Fifteenth Amendment, which was ratified in 1870 to secure the right to vote regardless of "race, color, or previous condition of servitude."

Frederick Douglass would spend the final decades of his life fighting such injustices. "If my wishes could be allowed to dictate my speech," he told an audience in 1888, "I would tell you that everything is lovely with the Negro in the South . . . that he is secure in his liberty; that he is tried by a jury of his peers when accused of a crime; that he is no longer subject to lynch law."[6] But the truth compelled Douglass to report something far bleaker about the condition of black Americans. "At no time since the abolition of slavery," he warned, "has there been more cause for alarm on this account than at this juncture in our history."[7]

It would be the last great battle of his life, and Douglass utilized every weapon at his disposal. He spoke out, wielded his pen, encouraged resistance. "Yes, let us have peace, but let us have liberty, law, and justice first," he declared, urging the federal government, including the federal courts, to fulfill its basic responsibility to safeguard the life, liberty, and property of every person under its authority. "Let us have the Constitution, with its thirteenth, fourteenth, and fifteenth amendments, fairly interpreted, faithfully executed, and cheerfully obeyed."[8] Tragically, he met with very limited success. Despite the best efforts of Douglass and others, Reconstruction ultimately gave way to Jim Crow.

It would fall to a new generation of civil rights activists, many inspired and guided by Douglass's words and deeds, to carry on the fight into the next century.

"No State . . . Shall Abridge"

The trouble started right away. In August 1865 a Mississippi convention instructed the state legislature to pass new laws guarding "against any evils that may arise from [the slaves'] sudden emancipation."[9] The state soon revealed precisely what sort of "evils" it was really worried about. "Every freedman, free negro, and mulatto," declared the Mississippi Black Code, must provide written evidence every January of a "lawful home or employment" or else run the risk of being arrested for vagrancy, a catchall offense that allowed state officials to sentence them to forced labor, a punishment that was sometimes carried out on the very same plantations on which these prisoners had once been held as slaves.[10] Around the same time, in Alabama, the legal definition of vagrancy was expanded to cover any "laborer or servant who loiters away his time."[11] That vague language offered a handy pretext for the authorities to arrest pretty much any African American adult they wanted, with a sentence of forced labor sure to follow. Through these and related machinations, those states sought to effectively reshackle many of their recently freed slaves. Other states quickly followed suit.

The right to earn a living was similarly besieged. One municipal ordinance in Louisiana, for example, declared that every "negro or freedman" must be "in the regular service of some white person or former owner."[12] In South Carolina, aspiring black shopkeepers and peddlers were required to persuade a local (white) official of their "skill and fitness."[13] Needless to say, that official permission was not readily granted. Likewise, in North Carolina, the sale of any object worth ten dollars or more required a white witness if either party to the sale was black. This made all manner of commercial activity difficult, if not impossible, for many blacks throughout many parts of the state. Similarly, in Opelousas, Louisiana, it became illegal for blacks to "sell, barter, or exchange any articles of merchandise" without the permission of local authorities. Under that same ordinance, blacks were prohibited from renting or keeping a house "within the limits of the town under any circumstances," with the further stipulation that "any one thus offending shall be ejected and compelled to find an employer or leave the town within twenty-four hours."[14]

In addition to gutting economic freedom, the Black Codes also shredded the right to self-defense. In Florida, for instance, it was made "unlawful for any Negro, mulatto, or person of color to own, use, or keep in possession or under control any bowie-knife, dirk, sword, firearms, or ammunition of any kind," without first obtaining the permission of local authorities.[15] Once again, such official permission was not readily granted. Mississippi's Black Code simply decreed that "no freedman, free Negro, or mulatto . . . shall keep or carry firearms of any kind."[16]

These oppressive measures all shared one overarching goal: to strip black Americans of their constitutional rights so that slavery, or a regime very much like it, could be reimposed. As Alexander Dunlap, a black resident of Williamsburg, Virginia, observed of the various forces arraying against him and his community in early 1866, "We feel in danger of our lives, of our property, and of everything else."[17]

Such outrages did not go unnoticed in Washington. When the Republican-controlled Congress opened its thirty-ninth session in December 1865, it began fashioning a series of responses. First came a new batch of federal legislation aimed at shoring up the imperiled civil rights of black Americans. The most significant such measure was the Civil Rights Act of 1866, which was enacted in April over the veto of President Andrew Johnson. It declared that all persons born on American soil are U.S. citizens and that all such citizens "of every race and color . . . shall have the same right, in every state and territory . . . to make and enforce contracts, to sue, be parties, and give evidence, to inherit, purchase, lease, sell, hold and convey real and personal property, and to full and equal benefit of all laws and proceedings for the security of persons and property, as is enjoyed by white citizens."[18]

The authors and supporters of the Civil Rights Act understood this legislation to serve a dual function, one that (a) protected fundamental rights from state abuse and (b) required the states to guarantee equal treatment under the law to all citizens regardless of race. In the words of the Republican congressman James Wilson of Iowa, who sponsored and managed the Civil Rights Act in the House of Representatives, "Citizens of the United States, as such, are entitled to possess and enjoy the great fundamental civil rights which it is the true office of Government to protect, and to equality in the exemptions of the law."[19]

According to Senator Lyman Trumbull of Illinois, the Republican leader who introduced and managed the legislation in the Senate, the Civil Rights Act protected "those inherent, fundamental rights which belong to free citizens or free men in all countries, such as the rights enumerated in this bill, and they belong to them in all the states of the union."[20] The Republican congressman William Lawrence of Ohio made a similar point, telling the House of Representatives that under the Civil Rights Act, "there are certain absolute rights which pertain to every citizen, which are inherent, and of which a state cannot constitutionally deprive him."[21]

What absolute rights did the Civil Rights Act protect? "Every citizen," Lawrence explained, "has the absolute right to live, the right of personal security, personal liberty, and the right to acquire and enjoy property. These are rights of citizenship. As necessary incidents of these absolute rights," he continued, "there are others, as the right to make and enforce contracts, to purchase, hold, and enjoy property, and to share the benefit of all laws for the security of person and property."[22]

This sweeping legislation did have its critics. The Democratic senator Willard Saulsbury of Delaware, for instance, objected to the Civil Rights Act because it would give blacks "every security for the protection of person and property which a white man has," including the right of armed self-defense. Saulsbury did not like the sound of that. "In my state for many years," he said, "there has existed a law of the state based upon and founded in its police power, which declared that free negroes shall not have possession of firearms or ammunition. This bill proposes to take away from the states this police power."[23]

President Andrew Johnson also complained about the loss of state power in his veto message to Congress. "Hitherto every subject embraced in the enumeration of rights contained in this bill has been considered as exclusively belonging to the States," Johnson wrote. "They are matters which in each State concern the domestic conditions of its people, varying in each according to its own peculiar circumstances and the safety and well-being of its own citizens."[24] To allow the Civil Rights Act to pass, Johnson declared, would be a "stride toward centralization."[25] He refused to sign it.

So, Congress went ahead and passed the law over Johnson's veto. "To be a citizen of the United States carries with it some rights," Senator Trumbull shot back in response to the president's objections. They are "inalienable rights, belonging to every citizen of the United States, as such, no matter where he may be." According to Trumbull, "The right of American citizenship means something."[26]

Several months later, that same Congress passed the legislation that would become the Fourteenth Amendment to the Constitution. A landmark provision, the Fourteenth Amendment began by settling the debate over black citizenship once and for all. "All persons born or naturalized in the United States, and subject to the jurisdiction thereof," the amendment declared, "are citizens of the United States and of the State wherein they reside." With those words, the Fourteenth Amendment formally overturned the Supreme Court's infamous 1857 ruling in *Dred Scott v. Sandford*, which held that persons of African descent could never be U.S. citizens. That pivotal language in the amendment was introduced by the Republican senator Jacob Howard of Michigan, a member of the congressional Joint Committee on Reconstruction and the amendment's floor manager. "This amendment I have offered," Howard told the Senate, "is simply declarative of what I regard as the law of the land already, that every person born within the limits of the United States, and subject to their jurisdiction, is by virtue of natural law and national law a citizen of the United States."[27]

Having resolved the matter of citizenship, the Fourteenth Amendment then turned to the business of rights. "No State," the amendment continued, "shall make or enforce any law which shall abridge the privileges or immunities of citizens of the United States; nor shall any State deprive any person of life, liberty, or property, without due process of law; nor deny to any person within its jurisdiction the equal protection of the laws." That consequential language was drafted primarily by the Republican congressman John Bingham of Ohio. He, too, was a member of the Joint Committee on Reconstruction; he was also an accomplished constitutional lawyer to boot.

The purpose of the Fourteenth Amendment, Bingham told the House of Representatives, was to provide a constitutional check against the "many instances of State injustice and oppression" that had occurred both before and after the Civil War. The amendment would do this by securing "the privileges or immunities of all the citizens of the Republic and the inborn rights of every person within its jurisdiction whenever the same shall be abridged or denied by the unconstitutional actions of any State."[28]

What did Bingham mean by the privileges or immunities of citizens? He meant individual rights, particularly the kind of individual rights that were associated with the Declaration of Independence and the Constitution, as well as the kind that were linked with the broader natural-rights philosophy that gave rise to both of those documents. "The provisions of the Constitution guaranteeing rights, privileges, and immunities to citizens of the United States," Bingham explained to the House of Representatives, included a host of fundamental liberties, such as those "chiefly defined in the first eight amendments to the Constitution" as well as the "constitutional liberty . . . to work in an honest calling and contribute by your toil in some sort to the support of yourself, to the support of your fellowmen, and to be secure in the enjoyment of the fruits of your toil."[29]

Senator Howard made a closely related point while shepherding the Fourteenth Amendment through the Senate. The amendment was necessary, Howard explained, because the "mass of privileges, immunities, and rights" secured by the Constitution "do not operate in the slightest degree as a restraint or prohibition upon State legislation."[30] Howard was alluding in part to the Supreme Court's 1833 decision in the case of *Barron v. Baltimore*, in which Chief Justice John Marshall held that the Bill of Rights "must be understood as restraining the power of the General Government, not as applicable to the States."[31] In other words, according to the holding in

Barron, the Fourth Amendment right to be free from unreasonable searches and seizures (to take just one example) did not apply against state or local governments—the amendment applied solely against federal authorities. The First Amendment, of course, was actually explicit about this fact, specifying that it was "Congress" that "shall make no law."

Howard was also alluding to what were known as the police powers of the states, which were the long-standing powers of local governments to enact regulations in the name of public health, welfare, or safety. That vast regulatory authority was traditionally understood to be immune from congressional oversight and free from federal judicial review. The Fourteenth Amendment, however, would change all of that. The amendment's purpose, Howard told the Senate, was "to restrict the power of the States and compel them at all times to respect these great fundamental guarantees."[32]

What "great fundamental guarantees" and what "mass of privileges, immunities, and rights" would the Fourteenth Amendment now protect? At a minimum, Howard told the Senate, it would protect those rights that were either mentioned or acknowledged in Justice Bushrod Washington's influential 1823 circuit court opinion in the case of *Corfield v. Coryell*, in which Justice Washington remarked that "it would be perhaps more tedious than difficult to enumerate" the full extent of the privileges and immunities of Americans. Despite the risk of tedium, however, Washington did specify a few, including "protection by the government; the enjoyment of life and liberty, with the right to acquire and possess property of every kind, and to pursue and obtain happiness and safety." All things, in sum, that "are, in their nature, fundamental; which belong, of right, to the citizens of all free governments."[33]

But that was not the end of it. In addition "to these privileges and immunities, whatever they may be—for they are not and cannot be fully defined in their extent and precise nature," Howard said, after quoting extensively from Washington's opinion in *Corfield*, "to these should be added the personal rights guaranteed and secured by the first eight amendments of the Constitution."[34] In other words, the Privileges or Immunities Clause secured from state infringement both those rights spelled out in the Bill of Rights as well as other, unenumerated rights that "are not and cannot be fully defined."

Once again, there were objections. The Fourteenth Amendment's opponents recognized its vast libertarian sweep and did their best to prevent it from being enshrined in the Constitution. "All the rights we have under the laws of the country are embarked under the definition of privileges and immunities," protested Democratic representative Andrew Jackson Rogers of New Jersey. "The right to marry is a privilege. The right to contract is a privilege.... I hold if that ever becomes a part of the fundamental law of the land it will prevent any State from refusing to allow anything to anybody embraced under this term of privileges and immunities."[35]

Speaking in Albany, New York, Frederick Douglass directed a few remarks at such opponents. Our "Democratic friends," he said, "are in a state of honest alarm" about the Fourteenth Amendment and the new limits that it places on state authority. "We ought to say a word of comfort to them." Perhaps they would feel better if they were told that "Jefferson wrote the Fourteenth Amendment," Douglass said. "That amendment is but the carrying out of Democratic doctrine—that all men are created equal, and have the inalienable right to life, liberty, and the pursuit of happiness."[36] Who could possibly object to that?

"A Vain and Idle Enactment"

On April 30, 1866, Chief Justice Salmon P. Chase wrote a letter to his Supreme Court colleague Justice Stephen Field about the proposal then pending before Congress to add the Fourteenth Amendment to the Constitution. One of the goals of the amendment, Chase observed, was "prohibiting the States from interfering with the rights of citizens." That worried him. Was it too radical a goal for moderates to support? "Will not these propositions," Chase wrote, "be received with some alarm by those who, though opponents of succession or nullification, yet regard the real rights of the States as essential to the proper working of government?" He added, "I do not myself think that any of the proposed amendments will be likely to have injurious effects."[37]

Two years later the Fourteenth Amendment was ratified and became a permanent part of the constitutional firmament. And just as Chase had described it, the new amendment prohibited the states from interfering with the rights of citizens. "No State," it declared, "shall make or enforce any law which shall abridge the privileges or immunities of citizens of the United States; nor shall any State deprive any person of life, liberty, or property, without due process of law; nor deny to any person within its jurisdiction the equal protection of the laws."

Chase's worries also proved accurate. When the first Fourteenth Amendment case was decided by the Supreme Court a few years later, a majority of Chase's own colleagues put state power before individual rights.

At issue in the *Slaughter-House Cases* of 1873 was an act of the Louisiana legislature that both established a central slaughterhouse for the city of New Orleans and granted a private corporation the exclusive authority to operate that facility for a period of twenty-five years. On the surface, the law had the appearance of an ordinary public health or safety measure. It required the inspection of all animals before slaughter, for example, and also required that all slaughtering be done downstream from the city, so as to avoid polluting the city's water supply. Such requirements undoubtedly served a public health or safety purpose. But what about the grant of an exclusive monopoly to a state-chartered corporation? How did *that* benefit the public? Was it not, in reality, just another instance of corruption and special-interest favoritism? The law, upon closer examination, did look a bit unsavory. As the historian Charles Lofgren has written, "Legislative bribery had greased passage of the law, with its most immediate beneficiaries—the seventeen participants in the corporation it established—adroitly distributing shares of stock and cash."[38]

There was also a constitutional problem. According to the hundreds of local butchers whose economic livelihoods were now at risk, the state's slaughterhouse monopoly law violated their right to earn a living, which, they insisted, was among the privileges or immunities of citizenship now under the protection of the Fourteenth Amendment. Organized as the Butchers' Benevolent Association, these malcontents filed suit, taking the case all the way up to the Supreme Court.

Their principal argument was that the Fourteenth Amendment had revolutionized the relationship between citizens and the states, placing a host of previously permissible state regulations on the judicial chopping block. Prior to the 1868 ratification of the Fourteenth Amendment, the butchers and their lawyer told the Supreme Court, "the rights of conscience, of speech, of labor, of intercourse and liberty, and security, were scarcely protected by the Constitution of the United States from State legislation." Similarly, before 1868, the Bill of Rights "was limited to declaring a protection against federal legislation or aggression," leaving the states alone. But now, with the Fourteenth Amendment securely in place, the situation was transformed, with citizens having "the safeguard of the power of the entire nation" behind them. "Conscience, speech, publication, security, occupation, freedom, and whatever else is essential to liberty, or is proper as an attribute of citizenship," argued the Butchers' Benevolent Association and its counsel, "are now held under the guarantee of the Constitution of the United States."[39] They urged the Supreme Court to strike down the slaughterhouse monopoly.

Charles Allen—the lawyer representing that state-sanctioned corporate monopoly, which was known as the Crescent City Live-Stock Landing and Slaughter-House Company—agreed that the case turned on the meaning of the Fourteenth Amendment. "There is no provision of the Constitution, prior to the 14th Amendment, which this charter can be supposed to violate," Allen observed in his brief to the Supreme Court.[40] But he disagreed entirely with the butchers about what the new amendment actually meant when it came to the regulatory authority of state lawmakers.

"The power of a State is complete, unqualified, and exclusive in relation to all those powers which relate to merely municipal legislation or internal police," Allen told the court. "The legislature is the sole and exclusive judge of whether a statute is reasonable, and for the benefit of the people."[41] The slaughterhouse monopoly, in other words, trumped the Fourteenth Amendment.

Thomas J. Durant, counsel for the state of Louisiana, echoed that argument in his brief to the court. Once a state legislature "judges that the interests of society will be better promoted by making such rights the exclusive privilege of a few, or of the State itself," he insisted, "this private right must yield to the public good."[42]

Several months later, the Supreme Court sided with the state and its corporate beneficiaries, upholding the Louisiana law by a margin of five votes to four. To interpret the Fourteenth Amendment as a federal shield in this case, declared the majority opinion of Justice Samuel Miller, "would constitute this court a perpetual censor upon all legislation of the States, on the civil rights of their own citizens." Miller would have no part of that. "The power here exercised" by Louisiana, Miller maintained, "has been, up to the present period in the constitutional history of this country, always conceded to belong to the States." For the court to rule otherwise, he insisted, would "fetter and degrade the State governments."[43]

As for the Privileges or Immunities Clause, Miller's interpretation essentially rewrote that constitutional safeguard out of existence. The clause was no broad charter of national freedom, he insisted. Instead, it should be seen as merely recognizing a small handful of federal privileges, such as "the right to use the navigable waters of the United States" and the right to visit the seat of the federal government.[44] The preexisting police powers of Louisiana, he declared, as well as those of every other state, remained fully intact.

It was exactly what Chief Justice Salmon P. Chase had feared back in 1866. Justice Miller cared more about the authority of the states than he did about the purposes of the Fourteenth Amendment.

Writing in dissent, Justice Stephen Field shook his head in disbelief. "It is to me a matter of profound regret that [the monopoly's] validity is recognized by a majority of this court," he wrote, "for by it the right of free labor, one of the most sacred and imprescriptible rights of man, is violated."[45] The whole point of the Fourteenth Amendment, Field wrote, was to protect the civil rights of U.S. citizens from state infringement, and "clearly among these must be placed the right to pursue a lawful employment in a lawful manner."[46] To be sure, Field acknowledged, Louisiana remained in possession of a legitimate police power that "extends to all regulations affecting the health, good order, morals, peace, and safety of society." But the slaughterhouse monopoly at issue did not satisfy any such criteria. It was "a mere grant" of special privilege to a politically connected corporation "by which the health of the city is in no way promoted."[47]

Field's dissent rejected Miller's legal analysis on every point. Just look at the historical evidence, Field wrote, such as the congressional debates over both the Civil Rights Act and the Fourteenth Amendment. Those debates made it clear that the framers of the Privileges or Immunities Clause wanted to impose significant new limits on the authority of the states. Yet thanks to Miller's ahistorical reasoning, the clause was now reduced to "a vain and idle enactment, which accomplished nothing and most unnecessarily excited Congress and the people upon its passage."[48] The court, Field concluded, had just committed a grievous mistake of judgment.

Unsurprisingly, given the content of his 1866 letter, Chief Justice Chase joined Field's dissent. Although he never publicly explained his stance in the *Slaughter-House Cases*, Chase's reasoning is not hard to fathom. A veteran antislavery lawyer and activist, Chase had long denounced slavery as "a power antagonistic to free labor."[49] Yet here was a majority of Chase's own court denying that the Fourteenth Amendment offered any substantive protections for free-labor principles. Of course Chase would have dissented from that. As biographer John Niven has explained, Chase "saw in the argument of [the Butchers' Benevolent Association] a means of strengthening the protection the Fourteenth Amendment afforded to the civil rights of blacks."[50]

Had he been a member of the Supreme Court, Frederick Douglass would have joined Field's dissent too. The *Slaughter-House* decision was "folly," Douglass wrote in an 1874 letter to Gerrit Smith. The Fourteenth Amendment clearly forbids the states from infringing on the civil rights of U.S. citizens. But now, thanks to this ruling, "the nation affirms, the State denies and there is no progress," Douglass observed. "The true doctrine is one nation, one country, one citizenship and one law for all the people."[51] As for what Field's dissent called "the right of free labor," Douglass had been championing that idea for years. "What is freedom?" Douglass once said. "It is the right to choose one's own employment. Certainly, it means that, if it means anything."[52]

"Badges and Incidents"

Bad as it was, the *Slaughter-House* decision was only the beginning. Three years later, the Supreme Court slammed the federal courthouse door shut on the victims of racist domestic terrorism.

The case of *United States v. Cruikshank* had its origins in the bitter fallout from the 1872 statewide elections in Louisiana. In Grant Parish, where Democrats and Republicans each laid competing claims to local office, the political fighting soon turned violent. In April 1873 an armed white mob with links to a local Democratic faction attacked the courthouse located in the town of Colfax, where hundreds of African Americans, including a black militia that supported the Republicans, had gathered in support of the local government. "The details are horrible," reported James R. Beckwith, the U.S. attorney in New Orleans, in a telegram that he sent to Attorney General George H. Williams in Washington DC. "The Democrats (white) of Grant Parish attempted to oust the incumbent parish officers by force and failed." Several days later, the assailants returned in greater numbers and launched a murderous assault. "The courthouse was fired and the negroes slaughtered as they left the burning building, after resistance ceased," Beckwith stated. "Sixty-five negroes terribly mutilated were found near the ruins of the courthouse. Thirty, known to have been taken prisoner, are said to have been shot after the surrender, and thrown in the river."[53] In the words of one historian, the Colfax massacre, as the event came to be known, was "the single bloodiest act of carnage in all of Reconstruction."[54]

Beckwith ran the investigation and prosecuted a number of the participants, including three of the massacre's ringleaders: William J. Cruikshank, William D. Irwin, and John P. Hadnot. He charged them with violating the Enforcement Act of 1870, a federal law aimed at curbing the activities of the Ku Klux Klan and related groups. Among others things, the Enforcement Act made it illegal for "two or more persons" to "band or conspire together . . . to injure, oppress, threaten, or intimidate any citizen with intent to prevent or hinder his free exercise and enjoyment of any right or privilege granted or secured to him by the Constitution or laws of the United States." Specifically, Cruikshank, Irwin, and Hadnot were charged with conspiring to prevent "certain citizens of African descent ... from (1) peaceably assembling together, (2) bearing arms, (3) enjoying life and liberty."[55]

The lawyers for those three defendants moved to get the case thrown out. There were no federal crimes to prosecute here, the defense team argued, because "the power to protect the lives, liberties and property of their citizens, while within the limits of the State," was a power that rested solely in the hands of that state. The authority to prosecute such local matters "was not granted to the Federal Government."[56] For example, the defense lawyers maintained, even if the white mob had forcibly disarmed the law-abiding black militia members, that was still not a federal crime, because "the right to bear arms, if it be a right, is a matter to be regulated and controlled by the State, as each State may deem best for itself."[57]

To support this argument, the defense lawyers cited "a case recently decided by the Supreme Court" that spelled out what "rights, privileges, immunities and protection" individuals "may claim, as citizens of the United States."[58] They were referring to the *Slaughter-House Cases*, in which "it will be seen that the right to bear arms is not enumerated among the rights of a citizen of the United States. Nor, is the right to assemble."[59] In effect, the defense team argued, the *Slaughter-House* precedent nullified the federal case against Cruikshank, Irwin, and Hadnot.

The Supreme Court, to the horror of Frederick Douglass and most other supporters of Reconstruction, ultimately agreed with the defense. "The people must look to the States" for the vindication of their rights in matters such as this, declared the majority opinion of Chief Justice Morrison Waite.[60] That went for alleged violations of both the First Amendment's guarantee of the right to assemble, Waite wrote, as well as for the Second Amendment's guarantee of the right to keep and bear arms, which leaves "the people to look [to the states] for their protection against any violation by their fellow-citizens of the rights it recognizes."[61] In fact, the chief justice declared, none of the individual liberties that are listed in the Bill of Rights were "intended to limit the powers of the State governments in respect to their own citizens, but to operate upon the National government alone."[62]

The *Cruikshank* precedent would stay on the books for decades to come. In fact, the Supreme Court did not get around to recognizing the First Amendment as a limit on the powers of the states (applied via the Fourteenth Amendment) until the 1925 case of *Gitlow v. New York*. As for the Second Amendment, the court did not recognize it as a limit on the states (again applied via the Fourteenth Amendment) until the 2010 case of *McDonald v. Chicago*.

Six years after *Cruikshank*, the Supreme Court dealt Reconstruction yet another devastating blow, this time by ruling the Civil Rights Act of 1875 unconstitutional. That 1883 decision, known as the *Civil Rights Cases*, centered on Congress's efforts to stamp out racial segregation in places of public accommodation via its authority under Section 5 of the Fourteenth Amendment, which granted Congress the "power to enforce, by appropriate legislation, the provisions of this article." According to the terms of the 1875 Civil Rights Act, every U.S. citizen was entitled to "full and equal enjoyment of the accommodations, advantages, facilities and privileges of inns, public conveyances on land and water, theaters and other places of public amusement, subject only to the conditions and limitations established by law, and applicable alike to citizens of any race or color, regardless of any previous condition of servitude."[63]

Among the plaintiffs in the *Civil Rights Cases* was a former enslaved woman named Sallie J. Robinson. On May 22, 1879, she bought a first-class ticket to ride on the Memphis and Charleston Railroad from Grand Junction, Tennessee, to Lynchburg, Virginia. Shortly after boarding the train, however, a conductor refused to let Robinson enter the first-class "ladies' car." As Robinson's lawyer, William M. Randolph, argued to the Supreme Court, if the railroad company "wishes to justify the denial [of a first-class seat]," then the Civil Rights Act mandates that the company must "prove that the denial was for *some reason*, and that *such reason* was in its nature

applicable to citizens of every race and color, regardless of any previous condition of servitude, and further, that such reason was by
law applicable to all such citizens."[64] But the company could prove
no such thing, Randolph continued, because the conductor had
turned Robinson away from the first-class car solely because of her
race and color. That, the lawyer maintained, was a clear-cut violation of the terms of the Civil Rights Act.

The Supreme Court took a different view. According to the majority opinion of Justice Joseph Bradley, the Civil Rights Act of 1875
was unconstitutional because Congress lacked the authority to regulate this sort of private behavior. Under the Fourteenth Amendment, the court said, Congress may only "provide modes of redress
against the operation of State laws, and the action of State officers
executive or judicial, when these are subversive of the fundamental rights specified in the amendment."[65] What Congress could not
do under the amendment, the court continued, was regulate wholly
private activity that did not involve any state law or state actor. In
short, Sallie J. Robinson, and other plaintiffs like her, were not entitled to any help from the federal authorities.

Writing in dissent, Justice John Marshall Harlan accused the majority of shortchanging not only the Fourteenth Amendment but the
Thirteenth Amendment as well. That constitutional provision, Har-
land wrote, which abolished the institution of slavery in 1865, also
abolished the "badges and incidents" of slavery, which he defined
as "all discrimination against [black Americans], because of their
race, in respect of such civil rights as belong to freemen of other
races."[66] What that meant in practice, Harlan insisted, was that Congress "may enact laws to protect that people against the deprivation,
because of their race, of any civil rights granted to other freemen in
the same State; and such legislation may be of a direct and primary
character, operating upon States, their officers and agents, and, also,
upon, at least, such individuals and corporations as exercise public
functions," a category that plainly included the owners and operators of a railroad company.[67]

To say the least, Frederick Douglass preferred Harlan's dissent
over Bradley's majority opinion. The Fourteenth Amendment was

"meant to protect the newly enfranchised citizen from injustice and wrong, not merely from a State, but from the individual members of a State," Douglass maintained. "It meant to give him the protection to which his citizenship, his loyalty, his allegiance, and his services entitled him." Yet "this meaning, this purpose, and this intention, is now declared unconstitutional and void, by the Supreme Court."[68] The ruling was a travesty, Douglass argued; it was an outrage.

Douglass was also incensed by the political affiliation of the opinion's author. "Had the bench been composed of Democratic judges some such a decision might have come upon us without producing any very startling effect," Douglass remarked.[69] But Justice Bradley, the author of the *Civil Rights Cases*, was a Republican appointee, nominated to the Supreme Court in 1870 by President Ulysses S. Grant. Nor was Bradley the only such judicial disappointment. Chief Justice Waite, the author of *United States v. Cruikshank*, was also a Grant appointee, nominated to the court in 1874 after the death of Chief Justice Salmon P. Chase. With friends like these on the bench, Douglass mused, who needed enemies?

But whether Douglass and his allies liked it or not, the damage was done. Thanks to the *Slaughter-House Cases*, *United States v. Cruikshank*, and the *Civil Rights Cases*, the Supreme Court effectively abdicated its role as a place of redress for victims of civil rights abuses in the post–Civil War period.

"This All-Important Right of Suffrage"

On April 22, 1870, the city of Albany, New York, played host to a grand celebration commemorating the recent ratification of the third and final amendment that would be added to the U.S. Constitution as a result of the Civil War. Tweddle Hall "was literally packed to suffocation with humanity," reported the *Albany Evening Journal*. "Even the lobbies and stairways were crowded with those unable to obtain an entrance to the main hall."[70] Inside the main hall it was practically pandemonium, as thousands of attendees raised their voices to the limits, singing the praises of the new Fifteenth Amendment, which guaranteed the right to vote regardless of "race, color, or previous condition of servitude."

Frederick Douglass was perhaps the happiest of all. "Today we are free American citizens," he told the crowd. "We have ourselves, we have a country, and we have a future in common with other men." Douglass was not exaggerating his views for rhetorical effect. As far as he was concerned, black suffrage was the single greatest achievement of the postwar period, a milestone accomplishment in the course of American history. "At last, at last," Douglass cheered, "the black man has a future."[71]

For Douglass, the fight for black suffrage had begun even before the Civil War was finished. On January 13, 1865, for example, with the prospects of the war's end just barely visible on the horizon, Douglass sketched out his vision for Reconstruction before a capacity crowd at New York City's Cooper Institute. "The fundamental principle of the reorganization of the South," he declared, must be "the absolute and complete enfranchisement of the entire black population of the South."[72]

Speaking in Boston two weeks later, Douglass again placed voting rights at the pinnacle of his agenda. "I have had but one idea for the last three years to present to the American people," Douglass said. "I am for the 'immediate, unconditional and universal' enfranchisement of the black man, in every State of the Union." How else, he asked, could black Americans secure their rights and make good their freedom, if not by making their presence felt at the ballot box? Without the right to vote, Douglass argued, an African American is merely "the slave of society, and holds his liberty as a privilege, not as a right. He is at the mercy of the mob, and has no means of protecting himself."[73]

And that was not the only reason why Douglass demanded the right to vote. It stands as a basic marker of citizenship, he told the crowd in Boston, as a signifier of one's full status as a member of the body politic. "If I were in a monarchical government," Douglass said, "where the few bore rule and the many were subject, there would be no special stigma resting upon me because I did not exercise the elective franchise." But here in the United States, "where universal suffrage is the rule . . . to rule us out is to make an exception, to brand us with the stigma of inferiority."[74] Douglass would not rest, he declared, until he had secured "this great, this all-important right of suffrage" for black Americans.[75]

Five years later, with the Fifteenth Amendment formally ratified, the great, all-important right was finally secured—or at least it was secured for black men. Women, of every race, would not obtain the constitutional right to suffrage until the 1920 ratification of the Nineteenth Amendment, which prohibited the denial or infringement of the right to vote "by the United States or by any State on account of sex."

The fight for the Fifteenth Amendment proved to be a bitter one. Not only did it force Douglass to square off, once more, against a number of familiar enemies, such as the many former slaveowners who now fought tooth and nail against black suffrage, but it also placed him in conflict with more than a few of his longtime friends. Most significantly, the debate over the Fifteenth Amendment put Douglass in direct opposition to one of his oldest allies, the pioneering feminist leader Elizabeth Cady Stanton.

Douglass and Stanton went way back. In fact, the two had worked closely together at one of the founding events of the American feminist movement, the storied Women's Rights Convention held in Seneca Falls, New York, on July 19–20, 1848. Of the one hundred participants who attended that landmark gathering, Douglass was one of just thirty-two men present, and he was the only black person involved. Stanton, who was born in Johnstown, New York, in 1815, was by far the convention's driving force. Already a leading participant in various reform-minded causes, including the abolitionist movement, Stanton would make the fight for women's rights her life's work.

After two days of debate and discussion, the Seneca Falls Convention issued its famous Declaration of Sentiments. Modeled directly on the American Declaration of Independence, this document championed the self-evident truths "that all men and women are created equal" and that women, the victims of "a long train of abuses and usurpations" by male-dominated government, have a "duty to throw off such a government, and to provide new guards for their future security."[76] In her history of the women's rights movement, Stan-

ton later reported that "the only resolution" contained in the Declaration of Sentiments "that was not unanimously adopted was the
ninth, urging the women of the country to secure to themselves the
elective franchise." That resolution, Stanton explained, was viewed
as far too extreme by some Seneca Falls attendees. They "feared a
demand for the right to vote would defeat others they deemed more
rational, and make the whole movement ridiculous."[77]

Stanton saw nothing ridiculous about it. Neither did Douglass,
who promptly joined her side in the sharp arguments that followed.
According to Stanton's account, the two of them together championed the idea "that the power to choose rulers and make laws was
the right by which all others could be secured." Eventually, they persuaded enough delegates to come over to their position, allowing
the voting rights resolution to carry the day "by a small majority."[78]

Two decades later, as the U.S. Congress first began contemplating
the legislative action that would culminate in the Fifteenth Amendment, the two veteran campaigners stood shoulder to shoulder
once again. In 1866 Stanton, along with the feminist leader Susan
B. Anthony and others, had formed a new group called the American Equal Rights Association. Its goal was to secure voting rights for
all American citizens, regardless of race or sex. Douglass was named
a vice president of their new group.

This time, however, the Stanton-Douglass alliance would not
endure for quite so long. As the debate over voting rights played out
on Capitol Hill, it became increasingly evident that the Fifteenth
Amendment was not going to include a provision granting suffrage
to women; the voting-rights amendment would apply only to men.
Once that outcome became clear, Stanton and Anthony turned hostile to the amendment and began wielding their considerable powers as writers, speakers, and activists in opposition to its passage
and ratification.

In December 1868, for example, Anthony wrote a letter to Gerrit Smith, urging the veteran antislavery leader to add his name to a
petition to Congress demanding that "there shall be no distinction
made between men and women" in "any change or amendment of
the Constitution you may propose, to extend or regulate suffrage."[79]

But Smith refused to sign any such petition. "Cheerfully, gladly can I sign a Petition for the enfranchisement of women," he wrote back. "But I cannot sign a paper against the enfranchisement of the negro man, unless at the same time woman shall be enfranchised. The removal of the disabilities of race is my first desire,—of sex, my second." The right of black suffrage, Smith argued, "if untrammeled" by competing claims for women's suffrage, "will soon be accomplished." After that, "its success will prepare the way for the accomplishment of the other."[80]

Meanwhile, in an editorial published that same month, Stanton came out swinging fiercely against the Fifteenth Amendment. "There is only one safe, sure way to build a government, and that is on the equality of all its citizens, male and female, black and white," she maintained.[81] The Fifteenth Amendment not only fell short of that necessary standard, Stanton believed, but it fatally undermined the bedrock principles that she had been fighting for since the Seneca Falls Convention.

Stanton was particularly incensed by the notion that women should take a backseat in the movement for equality. "We hear much high-sounding talk about 'saving the country,'" by rallying around the Fifteenth Amendment, she wrote. "But what is a country to the women who have no voice in the laws that govern them. What is a country [to those women] so long as all the fruit of their industry is stolen by their rulers?"[82]

Stanton then made an argument that drove the deepest of wedges between her and Frederick Douglass. Why, Stanton demanded, should educated white women be denied the vote while uneducated former slaves, not to mention uneducated immigrants, are granted access to the ballot box simply because they happened to be male? "Think of Patrick and Sambo and Hans and Young Tung," she wrote, employing common slurs for both blacks and several immigrant groups, "who never read the Declaration of Independence or Webster's spelling book." Why should they get the right to vote before someone like her? Would those "gentlemen who, on all sides, are telling us 'to wait until the negro is safe' be willing to stand aside and trust all *their* interests in hands like these?"[83] Dou-

glass was both offended and infuriated by Stanton's racist and elit-
ist language, and he let her know it.

The breaking point finally came in 1869 at the annual meeting of
the American Equal Rights Association, held in May at New York
City's Steinway Hall. "I must say that I do not see how anyone can
pretend that there is the same urgency in giving the ballot to women
as to the negro," Douglass told the gathering. "When women, because
they are women, are hunted down . . . when they are dragged from
their houses and hung upon lamp-posts . . . then they will have an
urgency to obtain the ballot equal to our own."[84]

"Is that not all true of black women?" demanded a voice from
the audience.[85]

"Yes," Douglass replied, "it is true of the black woman, but not
because she is a woman, but because she is black."[86] This was not
exactly a satisfactory response by Douglass, as it seemed to ignore the
fact that all women, regardless of race, faced the risk of sexual assault.

"Mr. Douglass talks about the wrongs of the negro," Susan B.
Anthony told the gathering a few minutes later. "But with all the
wrongs and outrages that he today suffers, he would not exchange
his sex and take the place of Elizabeth Cady Stanton."[87] In other
words, Anthony argued, Douglass knew deep down that Stanton and
Anthony had the better case. The pervasive subjugation of women
gave them every justification for demanding their liberty and equality now.

The American Equal Rights Association did not survive long
after that. A month later Stanton and Anthony split off to form a
new, competing group, the National Woman Suffrage Association,
which would focus exclusively on advancing the feminist cause.
"While we rejoice in every step toward putting an end, on this continent, to an aristocracy of color," the new group announced in a
resolution drafted by Stanton, "we repudiate the Fifteenth Amendment, because by its passage in Congress, the Republican Party propose to substitute an aristocracy of sex, the most odious distinction
in citizenship that has ever yet been proposed since Governments
had an existence."[88]

In time, Douglass would again collaborate with Stanton and

Anthony on behalf of women's rights. Sharing the stage with Stanton in 1888, for example, Douglass would proudly describe himself as "a radical woman suffrage man." The government must lift its "obstructive forces of fines and imprisonment and [its] obstructive uses out of the way, and let woman express her sentiments at the polls and in the government, equally," he declared. "Give her fair play and let her alone."[89] But that was in the future. For now, the struggle to secure ratification and enforcement of the Fifteenth Amendment was Douglass's top priority. Besides, Douglass figured, he had an even bigger problem than Stanton or Anthony to worry about. The fight for black suffrage had placed him on a collision course with none other than the president of the United States of America.

"No Friend of Our Race"

The way Frederick Douglass told it, he learned to distrust Andrew Johnson practically on sight. On March 4, 1865, Douglass was in Washington DC, one of the many thousands of people gathered in attendance for the second inauguration of President Abraham Lincoln. According to Douglass's account, he watched from the crowd as Lincoln conferred privately with Johnson, his vice president to be. "Mr. Lincoln touched Mr. Johnson and pointed me out to him," Douglass reported. "The first expression which came to [Johnson's] face, and which I think was the true index of his heart, was one of bitter contempt and aversion." Johnson quickly realized that Douglass was looking right back at him, so he "tried to assume a more friendly appearance." But there was no mistaking that original, unguarded expression of hostility. Douglass, according to his telling, then turned to his neighbor in the crowd and remarked, "Whatever Andrew Johnson may be, he certainly is no friend of our race."[90]

That prediction would prove all too accurate. Indeed, within less than a year of assuming the presidency after Lincoln's assassination, Johnson would emerge as such an enemy of Reconstruction that both radical and moderate Republicans were left gnashing their teeth in frustration (they also began contemplating the impeachment proceedings that they would eventually launch against Johnson in 1868). In the opening months of 1866 alone, for example,

Johnson vetoed the second Freedmen's Bureau Act, vetoed the Civil Rights Act, and denounced the Fourteenth Amendment as a constitutional deformity. In the words of historian Annette Gordon-Reed, Johnson "did everything he could to make sure blacks would never become equal citizens in the United States of America. Tragically, he was able to bring the full force and prestige of the American presidency to this effort."[91]

Johnson proved particularly hostile to the idea of extending voting rights to blacks. Once again, Douglass would be an eyewitness to Johnson's contempt and aversion. In February 1866 a delegation of civil rights leaders, including Douglass, secured a White House audience with the president. Their objective that day was to press the case for black suffrage. "Your noble and humane predecessor placed in our hands the sword to assist in saving the nation," Douglass said to Johnson, referring to Lincoln. "We hope that you, his able successor, will favorably regard the placing in our hands the ballot with which to save ourselves."[92]

Blacks had undeniably earned the right to vote, Douglass continued in his remarks to the president. And not only because of their contributions to the war effort. "The fact that we are the subjects of Government and subject to taxation, to volunteer in the service of the country, subject to being drafted, subject to bear the burdens of the State," Douglass maintained, "makes it not improper that we should ask to share in the privileges of this condition."[93]

Johnson coldly replied that he did not appreciate being "arraigned by some who can get up handsomely-rounded periods and deal in rhetoric, and talk about abstract ideas of liberty."[94] Then, having thus insulted Douglass and the others, the president got to the point. He was entirely opposed to extending voting rights to blacks, because it would cause "great injury to the white as well as the colored man." In Johnson's view, it might "commence a war of races," as he put it, if blacks and whites, with their shared history, were "thrown together at the ballot-box with this enmity and hate existing between them."[95]

Then, taking a step closer to Douglass, the president asked whether it would be "proper to force upon this [white] community, without their consent, the elective franchise, without regard to color, making it universal?" Johnson announced, "If a great majority of the people said no, I should consider it would be tyrannical in me to attempt to force such upon them without their will." After all, the president asked, does not the will of the majority deserve some respect? "Is there anything wrong or unfair in that?"

"A great deal that is wrong, Mr. President," Douglass replied with a tight smile, "with all respect."

But the president refused to budge, and the meeting came to an uncomfortable end. "It is the people of the States that must for themselves determine this thing," Johnson concluded. "I do not want to be engaged in a work that will commence a war of races."[96]

The delegation left the White House fuming. In a public response, written that same day and reprinted in newspapers around the country, Douglass unleashed a torrent of rebuke. The president's views "are entirely unsound and prejudicial to the highest interest of our race as well as our country at large," he wrote.[97] Johnson's approach would deny black Americans "all means of defence," while at the same time ensuring that whites continued to monopolize political power and influence. "Peace between races is not to be secured by degrading one race and exalting another, by giving power to one race and withholding it from another." Peace would only be secured, Douglass insisted, "by maintaining a state of equal justice between all classes."[98]

Douglass would have plenty more to say against the president in the days ahead. Johnson was the "embodiment of political treachery, meanness, baseness, ingratitude, the vilest of the vile, the basest of the base, the most execrable of the execrable of modern times," Douglass declared a year later in St. Louis, Missouri.[99] The president "is without principles or friends, for no men or set of men can be said to love Andrew Johnson," Douglass told a crowd in Philadelphia. Johnson, Douglass concluded, "shall go down to eternal infamy."[100]

The feeling was mutual. According to the president's private secretary, Johnson had cursed out "that d—d Douglass" after their February 1866 meeting, employing a racial slur while characterizing Douglass as the sort who "would sooner cut a white man's throat than not."[101]

Johnson remained staunchly opposed to black suffrage through-out his single term in office, never hesitating to use the bully pul-pit to rail against what he called "the subjugation of the States to negro domination."[102] Perhaps the lowest point came in December 1867, when Johnson delivered his third annual message to Congress. Employing nakedly racist language, Johnson attacked the proposed Fifteenth Amendment on the grounds that "negroes have shown less capacity for government than any other race of people." His argu-ment was that because blacks had proven themselves fundamen-tally incapable of self-government, they had no business exercising the right to vote under the U.S. Constitution.

Thankfully, that vile argument lost out in the end. On February 3, 1870, a little less than a year after Johnson vacated the White House, the Fifteenth Amendment was officially ratified.

"The Lynch Abomination"

In his third and final autobiography, *Life and Times of Frederick Dou-glass*, the great abolitionist confessed to suffering from a certain mel-ancholy in his later years. The end of slavery, "which had been the deepest desire and the great labor of my life," Douglass wrote, was also "slightly tinged with a feeling of sadness." This was because "I felt I had reached the end of the noblest and best part of my life; my school was broken up, my church disbanded."[103] Did Douglass still have anything to offer his country as the ferocious debates over slavery—and the bloody war that followed from them—gradually faded from the national memory? Was there any great cause to which he might devote the remaining days of his life?

There was. As the nineteenth century was reaching its conclusion, a horrifying new chapter in American race relations was beginning to unfold. Throughout the South, untold numbers of black persons were being tortured and killed by lynch mobs. To be sure, white supremacist violence against black Americans was nothing new. But the rise and widespread occurrence of lynching was still a shocking new development. And as the historian C. Vann Woodward has noted, it was "in the [1880s] and [1890s] that lynching attained the most staggering proportions ever reached in the history of that crime."[104]

If any cause in the late nineteenth century called out for the unique talents of Frederick Douglass, the fight against lynching was it.

But first Douglass required a thorough education in the reality of what was going on. Fortunately, he would find himself in the hands of the most capable teacher around. Ida B. Wells was born into slavery in Holly Springs, Mississippi, in 1862. At the age of twenty-two, she moved to Memphis, Tennessee, in order to work as a teacher. A few years later, she picked up her pen to work as a journalist and editor for the *Free Speech and Headlight*, a local black newspaper whose name would later be shortened to the *Free Speech*. In the years ahead, Wells's extraordinary work as an investigative reporter would galvanize the nation and help inspire a new wave of civil rights activism, including activism by Douglass himself.

On March 9, 1892, three black men—Thomas Moss, Calvin McDowell, and Henry Stewart—were lynched in Memphis. Coverage by the local white press suggested that the men got what they deserved, that they were lawless villains who threatened white society. Wells knew better and set out to prove it in the pages of the *Free Speech*. As her reporting demonstrated, the three victims were partners in a grocery store, known as the People's Grocery Company, that had opened for business in a neighborhood called the Curve. A white grocer already operated in the area, and he looked none too kindly on his new black competitors. The violence and brutality that followed was all rooted in that white grocer's racial animus.

It started when a schoolyard fight among local black and white children spilled over into a fistfight involving a number of their parents. In the aftermath, the white grocer began loudly blaming his black competitors for stirring up the racial conflict. Those unfounded accusations led to repeated threats of violence against the People's Grocery and its owners. Things finally came to a head one Saturday night. As Wells reported, "McDowell and his clerk were waiting on customers preparatory to closing" when suddenly "shots rang out in the back room of the store. The men stationed there [as guards] had seen several white men stealing through the rear door and fired on them without a moment's pause." That act of armed self-defense gave the local authorities all the excuse that they needed for a general clampdown on the area's black residents. "Over a hundred colored men were dragged from their homes and put in jail on suspicion," Wells noted, including the three business partners.[105] Two days later, a mob of armed whites removed Moss, McDowell, and Stewart from the jailhouse and proceeded to lynch them outside of town. "Thus, with the aid of the city and county authorities and the daily papers," Wells concluded, "that white grocer had indeed put an end to his rival Negro grocer as well as to his business."[106]

Wells's reporting would expose this and other vile episodes for the racist crimes that they were. "Eight Negroes lynched since last issue of the *Free Speech*," she wrote in one editorial. "Three charged with killing white men and five with raping white women. Nobody in this section believes the old thread-bare lie that Negro men assault white women."[107] Local whites, outraged by her reporting, responded with additional violence and, in the end, basically ran her out of town. On May 27, while Wells was traveling to New York City for a meeting with T. Thomas Fortune, the editor of the *New York Age*, which was then one of the country's most prominent black publications, a group of whites descended on the offices of the *Free Speech* and wrecked its printing equipment. "Well, we've been a long time getting you to New York, but now you are here I am afraid you will have to stay," Fortune told her after sharing the news of the *Free Speech*'s destruction.[108] Wells accepted that blunt assessment of her situation and signed on as a business partner and writer for the *New York Age*.

Her byline appeared a few weeks later on the front page of the June 25 issue. The article that followed not only laid bare the facts behind the recent spate of lynching in Memphis but also exposed the truth behind other such heinous crimes throughout the South. "Somebody must show that the Afro-American race is more sinned against than sinning, and it seems to have fallen upon me to do so," Wells would say of her reporting. "The awful death-roll that Judge Lynch is calling every week is appalling, not only because of the lives it takes . . . but because of the prejudice it fosters and the stain it places against the good name of a weak race."[109]

Frederick Douglass was among the many thousands who read her article in the *New York Age* with great interest. He was so awed by it, in fact, that he traveled to New York City from his home in Washington DC in order to discuss the matter with Wells in person. He told her "what a revelation of existing conditions this article had been to him," Wells reported. Incredibly, Douglass even told her that he himself had been fooled by the overwhelmingly racist slant of most mainstream accounts of the lynching epidemic and its causes. According to Wells, Douglass told her that "he had been troubled by the increasing number of lynchings, and had begun to believe it true that there was increasing lasciviousness on the part of Negroes."[110] It took Wells's groundbreaking journalism to set him straight.

"This was the beginning of a friendship," Wells later wrote, "which lasted until the day of his death, three years later." And she "never ceased to be thankful for this contact with him."[111] Douglass was thankful too. As the historian Leigh Fought has argued, Douglass was so impressed and heavily influenced by Wells and her work that he might well have viewed her as "his heir apparent in civil rights." After all, she was "imbued with every bit of the same fiery passion, intelligence, and independence as Douglass himself exhibited at her age." He would have found her "not so much a daughter-activist . . . but a female version of his younger self."[112]

Douglass was soon lending his own famous name and reputation in support of Wells's endeavors. He wrote letters of praise and introduction, helped organize speaking engagements for her, and also penned a short preface to her 1892 book, *Southern Horrors*, in which she expanded on her breakout *New York Age* story. "Let me give you thanks for your faithful paper on the lynch abomination now generally practiced in the South," Douglass wrote in that preface, before praising Wells for her "cool, painstaking fidelity" to the facts. "Brave woman! You have done your people and mine a service which can neither be weighed nor measured."[113]

Supplied with the intellectual ammunition first crafted by Wells, Douglass also enlisted himself in the antilynching fight. To say that "American law is now the shield of black and white alike" would be a "flagrant disregard of the truth," Douglass wrote in a widely circulated pamphlet. The truth was that barbaric mobs were "allowed to supersede courts of law" and "usurp the place of government." The truth was that blacks were being "tortured, shot, hanged, or burned to death on suspicion of crime and without ever seeing a judge, jury or advocate."[114] Lynching was more than just a horrific assault on its individual victims, Douglass stressed; it was a violation of justice, of due process, and of the very idea of constitutional government.

In addition to mounting a campaign of writings and speeches, Douglass also sought to lobby the federal government at its highest levels of power. As an elder statesman of the Republican Party, Douglass had little difficulty securing himself an appointment at the Republican-controlled White House. So there he went, in the hopes of convincing President Benjamin Harrison, a former Union colonel in the Civil War, to denounce lynching from the presidential bully pulpit and to throw the entire weight of his office behind a federal antilynching bill. Douglass "eloquently pleaded the case for anti-lynching legislation," reported Mary Church Terrell, a leader of the Colored Woman's League of Washington, who accompanied Douglass to the White House meeting. "He implored President Harrison to act immediately against the lynching evil."[115] Harrison, however, failed to take action.

Douglass, no stranger to an uphill fight, simply pressed on, making the case against lynching in every venue that was available to him. He was now in his midseventies, and his age was definitely starting to show. But the old radical had no intentions of slowing down. To the contrary, Douglass had every intention of going down swinging.

"There Would Be No Negro Problem"

Frederick Douglass delivered perhaps his definitive statement on the lynching epidemic before a capacity crowd at the Metropolitan AME Church in Washington DC on January 9, 1894. "Not a breeze comes to us now from the late rebellious States," he observed, "that is not tainted and freighted with negro blood."[116] Half a century before, he had published his first book, *Narrative of the Life of Frederick Douglass, an American Slave,* a work that established him both as a leader of the abolitionist movement and as one of the greatest Americans of his age, a tireless champion of what the Declaration of Independence called unalienable rights. Now, in the twilight of his career,

Douglass would stand up once more for the principles of liberty and equality to which he had devoted his life.

"I am here," he told the audience in Washington, "to speak for, and to defend, so far as I can do so within the bounds of truth, a long-suffering people, and one just now subject to much misinformation and persecution."[117] He then proceeded to set the record straight.

There are those who defended the act of lynching, Douglass observed, who said that these hideous assassinations were merely another form of frontier justice, who said that lynching was an understandable response from the white community in the face of rampant black criminality. But where, he demanded, was the proof of any such underlying criminal behavior among black Americans? The "negro's accusers," Douglass pointed out, "dare not confront him in a court of law and have their witnesses subjected to proper legal authority." Instead, they spread lies and innuendos, stoking public hysteria while carefully avoiding anything that resembled a deliberative legal process as they went about their murderous work. Furthermore, those same accusers had already "violated their oaths and cheated the negro out of his vote," just as they had "robbed and defrauded the negro systematically and persistently, and [had] boasted of it."[118] No impartial observer could possibly take the members of a lynch mob at their word. "I would not, and you would not," said Douglass, "convict a dog on such testimony."[119]

To make matters worse, he observed, these white vigilantes were being enabled by virtually every important institution in their communities, from the press to the police department to the pulpit. "The mobocratic murderers are not only permitted to go free, untried and unpunished, but are lauded and applauded as honorable men and good citizens, the guardians of Southern women."[120] That was the terrifying state of affairs now facing black Americans in significant parts of the country.

"I do not pretend that negroes are saints or angels," Douglass continued.[121] Black people sometimes break the law, just as white people sometimes do. But if an individual is guilty, he asserted, let that person's guilt be determined by a properly convened court of law, not by the howls of a racist throng. "What every honest man, black or white, should contend for," Douglass maintained, is that the accused "shall have the benefit of a legal investigation; that he shall be confronted by his accusers; and that he shall through proper counsel, be able to question his accusers in open court and in open day-light so that his guilt or innocence may be duly proved and established."[122] To accept anything less than that, he stressed, is to forfeit all pretense of justice and fair play.

In the past, when Douglass had spoken out against the other great evils facing black Americans, he had always managed to strike a note of optimism. "Notwithstanding the dark picture I have this day presented," he declared in his famous Fourth of July oration in 1852, "I do not despair of this country. There are forces in operation which must inevitably work the downfall of slavery."[123] Likewise, speaking in the aftermath of the Supreme Court's *Dred Scott* decision in 1857, Douglass reminded his audience of the extraordinary progress that the antislavery movement had already made in the face of equally steep hurdles. "Emancipation, they tell us, is a wild, delusive idea," Douglass remarked. And yet "the anti-slavery movement has, from first to last, suffered no abatement. It has gone forth in all directions, and is now felt in the remotest extremities of the Republic."[124] Even in the most desperate hour, Douglass would always counsel his fellow black Americans to take heart.

But Douglass did not sound quite so optimistic in 1894. Recent events had "shaken [his] faith in the nobility of the nation," he admitted. And he was not just referring to the horrors of lynching. "The Supreme Court has surrendered," Douglass observed. Both the Congress and the White House have gone cold in their support for the cause of civil rights. "I hope and trust all will come out right in the end," he said, "but the immediate future looks dark and troubled. I cannot shut my eyes to the ugly facts before me."[125]

Still, Douglass allowed that he was not entirely bereft of hope. "In old times when it was asked, 'How can we abolish slavery?'" Douglass observed, "The answer was 'Quit stealing.' The same is the solution of the Race problem to-day."[126] As he had done so many times before, Douglass returned to the bedrock liberal principles enshrined in America's founding documents. The race problem could be solved "by simply no longer evading the amendments of the Constitution," he maintained, "and no longer evading the claims of justice." If only the American people, and the government that represented them, would just live up to those principles, he said, "there would be no negro problem to vex the South, or to vex the nation."[127]

Douglass's speech that day in Washington, titled "Lessons of the Hour," was a slashing, soaring address. Later printed in pamphlet form, it would be widely circulated and read throughout the country. Sadly, it would also go down as one of the last great speeches of his long and storied career. A little over a year later, the great abolitionist would be in his grave.

Epilogue

A Legacy of Liberty

Frederick Douglass spent the last day of his life doing what he did best: fighting for freedom and equality. It was February 20, 1895, and the National Council of Women was holding a meeting in Washington DC. Douglass was there among the attendees, busily conferring with Susan B. Anthony, the veteran feminist leader with whom he had once sparred over the Fifteenth Amendment and its lack of support for women's suffrage. But that conflict was now long behind them, and Douglass was pleased to be laboring side by side once again with his old friend and ally. After all, as he liked to say, he was "a radical woman suffrage man."[1] As he told a Boston audience in 1888, "When I ran away from slavery, it was for myself; when I advocated emancipation, it was for my people; but when I stood up for the rights of woman, self was out of the picture, and I found a little glory in that."[2] It seems altogether fitting that Douglass's final public act would involve championing the glorious cause of women's rights.

He returned home in the early evening in order to get some rest and to have a bite of food before heading out again for another speaking engagement that night. But death found him first. One moment he was talking to his second wife, Helen (Pitts) Douglass, when suddenly he collapsed to his knees and then crumbled to the floor, felled by an apparent heart attack or perhaps by a stroke. He was seventy-seven years old.

As the news of his death spread, the tributes came pouring in. "Though born and reared in slavery," remarked the obituarist for the *New York Times*, Douglass "managed, through his own perseverance and energy, to win for himself a place that not only made him beloved by all members of his own race in America, but also won for himself the esteem and reverence of all fair-minded persons, both in this country and in Europe."[3] The *Times* of London largely echoed that assessment, describing Douglass's life as "singularly useful, not only to his race, but to the nation which at first refused him citizenship."[4] For Ida B. Wells, the fearless young journalist who would take up Douglass's mantle and carry on his legacy of agitation and activism into the next century, he was simply "the greatest man our race has produced in this 'land of the free and home of the brave.'"[5]

Over a century after his death, Frederick Douglass's star still burns brightly. His penetrating ideas about freedom, equality, and individualism continue to stand out for their clarity and originality. His forceful arguments against racism and collectivism still have the power to win any debate. "You are a man, and so am I," Douglass wrote to his old master, Thomas Auld, in an open letter first published in the *North Star* on September 3, 1848. "In leaving you, I took nothing but what belonged to me."[6] Has a more definitive indictment of slavery ever been written? Has a better distillation of the liberal principles coursing through the Constitution and Declaration of Independence ever been penned?

Through his words, his actions, and the extraordinary personal example that he set, Frederick Douglass helped to move his country a little bit closer toward liberty. If only more Americans—then and now—could say the same thing.

Acknowledgments

T hank you to my agent, Don Fehr, and to my editor, Tom Swanson, whose efforts and support made this book possible.

Thank you to my boss, Katherine Mangu-Ward, for her wise counsel and for giving me the opportunity to focus on book writing for a spell. Thanks also to the rest of the gang at *Reason* magazine, including Mike Alissi, Meredith Bragg, Elizabeth Nolan Brown, Brian Doherty, Jim Epstein, Nick Gillespie, Jon Graff, David Nott, Mike Riggs, Stephanie Slade, Peter Suderman, Jacob Sullum, Jesse Walker, Matt Welch, and Liz Wolfe.

Warm thanks to the wonderful staff at Columbia University's Butler Library, the New York Public Library, and the Library of Congress.

Endless love and thanks to my family: Trudie Root, Amy Root, Alex Root, Dan Root, Maria Root, Kellan Root, Katherine Ayala, Charlotte Kent, Tim Kent, Alexander Searing, Keith Searing, Trish Hickling, Rick McKim, and Ellen Mittenthal.

Finally, to Allison McKim, my partner in crime, meeting you was the best thing that ever happened to me. Thanks for everything.

Notes

Introduction

1. Wendell Philips Garrison and Garrison, *William Lloyd Garrison*, 3:88.
2. Douglass, *My Bondage and My Freedom*, 260–61.
3. Douglass, "Change of Opinion Announced," in *Frederick Douglass: Selected Speeches and Writings*, 173–74.
4. Douglass, "Change of Opinion Announced," 174.
5. Douglass, *My Bondage and My Freedom*, 292–93.
6. Douglass, "The Constitution and Slavery," in *Frederick Douglass: Selected Speeches and Writings*, 129.
7. Douglass, "Oath to Support the Constitution," in *Life and Writings*, 2:118–19.
8. Douglass, "The Meaning of July Fourth for the Negro," in *Life and Writings*, 2:202.
9. Douglass, "Oath to Support the Constitution," 118.
10. Douglass, "Meaning of July Fourth for the Negro," 202.
11. Douglass, "The Mission of the War," in *Life and Writings*, 3:403.
12. Douglass, *Frederick Douglass: Autobiographies*, 817.

1. "A Faithful Disciple"

1. Cong. Globe, 24th Cong., 2nd Sess. 162 (1837).
2. Cong. Globe, 24th Cong., 2nd Sess. 162 (1837), emphasis in the original.
3. Cong. Globe, 24th Cong., 2nd Sess. 162 (1837), emphasis in the original.
4. 12 Reg. Deb. 1966 (1835).
5. 12 Reg. Deb. 1966 (1835).
6. 12 Reg. Deb. 1967 (1835).
7. 12 Reg. Deb. 2005 (1835).
8. 12 Reg. Deb. 1973 (1835).
9. 12 Reg. Deb. 3757 (1836).
10. 12 Reg. Deb. 4053 (1836).

11. 12 Reg. Deb. 2001–2 (1835).

12. 13 Reg. Deb. 1588 (1837).

13. 13 Reg. Deb. 1599 (1837).

14. 13 Reg. Deb. 1620 (1837).

15. 13 Reg. Deb. 1633 (1837).

16. 13 Reg. Deb. 1665 (1837).

17. 13 Reg. Deb. 1673–74 (1837).

18. 13 Reg. Deb. 1733 (1837).

19. Douglass, "I Have Come to Tell You Something about Slavery," in *Frederick Douglass Papers*, ser. 1, 1:4.

20. Douglass, *Frederick Douglass: Autobiographies*, 16.

21. Douglass, *Frederick Douglass: Autobiographies*, 477.

22. Douglass, *My Bondage and My Freedom*, 63–64.

23. Douglass, *My Bondage and My Freedom*, 107.

24. Douglass, *My Bondage and My Freedom*, 107–8, emphasis in the original.

25. Douglass, *My Bondage and My Freedom*, 109.

26. Bingham, *Columbian Orator*, iii.

27. Stauffer and Gates, introduction to Douglass, *Portable Frederick Douglass*, xxiv.

28. Bingham, "Dialogue between a Master and Slave," in *Columbian Orator*, 240.

29. Douglass, *My Bondage and My Freedom*, 117.

30. Douglass, "My Slave Experience in Maryland," in *Frederick Douglass: Selected Speeches and Writings*, 12.

31. Douglass, "My Slave Experience in Maryland," 13.

32. William Lloyd Garrison, "To the Public," *Liberator*, January 1, 1831.

33. Douglass, *My Bondage and My Freedom*, 260.

34. Douglass, *My Bondage and My Freedom*, 202.

35. Douglass, *My Bondage and My Freedom*, 208.

36. Douglass, *My Bondage and My Freedom*, 256.

37. Fought, *Women in the World of Frederick Douglass*, 51.

38. Douglass, *My Bondage and My Freedom*, 260.

39. "Meeting in Faneuil Hall," *Liberator*, February 1, 1839.

40. "Token of Respect," *Liberator*, January 25, 1839.

41. "Munificent Donation," *Liberator*, January 25, 1839.

42. Pacificus, "Non-Resistance," *Liberator*, January 11, 1839.

43. William Lloyd Garrison, "Human Government," *Liberator*, January 25, 1839.

44. Douglass, "There Was a Right Side in the Late War," in *Frederick Douglass: Selected Speeches and Writings*, 629.

45. Douglass, *My Bondage and My Freedom*, 261.

46. Chapman, *William Lloyd Garrison*, 42.

47. Edmund Quincy to R. D. Webb, January 29, 1843, in Wendell Philips Garrison and Garrison, *William Lloyd Garrison*, 3:91.

48. Oliver Johnson, *William Lloyd Garrison and His Times*, 51–52.

49. Garrison, "To the Public," emphasis in the original.

50. May, *Some Recollections*, 36–37.

51. Oliver Johnson, *William Lloyd Garrison and His Times*, 60–61.

52. Chapman, *William Lloyd Garrison*, 48.

53. Douglass, *My Bondage and My Freedom*, 260.

54. William Lloyd Garrison, preface to Douglass, *Narrative of the Life*, iv.

55. William Lloyd Garrison, "Anti-Slavery Excursion to Cape Cod," *Liberator*, July 1, 1842.

56. Quoted in Wendell Philips Garrison and Garrison, *William Lloyd Garrison*, 3:19.

57. William Lloyd Garrison to Helen Eliza Garrison, August 9, 1847, in *Liberator*, August 20, 1847.

58. William Lloyd Garrison, "On the Constitution and the Union," *Liberator*, December 29, 1832, emphasis in the original.

59. Wendell Philips Garrison and Garrison, *William Lloyd Garrison*, 3:98.

60. Wendell Philips Garrison and Garrison, *William Lloyd Garrison*, 3:88.

61. Quincy to Webb, January 29, 1843, 88.

62. Wendell Philips Garrison and Garrison, *William Lloyd Garrison*, 3:111, emphasis in the original.

63. Wendell Philips Garrison and Garrison, *William Lloyd Garrison*, 3:99.

64. William Lloyd Garrison, "Address to the Friends of Freedom and Emancipation in the United States," *Liberator*, May 31, 1844.

65. Hofstadter, *American Political Tradition*, 181.

66. Irving H. Bartlett, "The Persistence of Wendell Phillips," in Duberman, *Antislavery Vanguard*, 102–3.

67. Phillips, *Constitution, a Pro-Slavery Compact*, 6.

68. Phillips, *Constitution, a Pro-Slavery Compact*, 7, emphasis in the original.

69. Phillips, *Constitution, a Pro-Slavery Compact*, 7.

70. Phillips, *Constitution, a Pro-Slavery Compact*, 6.

71. *Federalist*, no. 42 (James Madison), in Hamilton, Madison, and Jay, *Federalist Papers*, 264.

72. *Federalist*, no. 54 (James Madison), in Hamilton, Madison, and Jay, *Federalist Papers*, 337.

73. Douglass, *My Bondage and My Freedom*, 291.

74. Douglass, "Farewell Speech to the British People," in *Frederick Douglass: Selected Speeches and Writings*, 56.

75. Douglass, "Farewell Speech to the British People," 58.

76. Douglass, "American Slavery," in *Life and Writings*, 1:274–75.

77. Douglass to Thomas Van Rensselaer, May 18, 1847, in *Frederick Douglass: Selected Speeches and Writings*, 85.

78. Douglass, *My Bondage and My Freedom*, 266, emphasis in the original.

79. William Lloyd Garrison, "Declaration of Sentiments of the American Anti-Slavery Society," in Ruchames, *Abolitionists*, 79.

80. Douglass, *Frederick Douglass: Autobiographies*, 65.

81. Douglass, *Frederick Douglass: Autobiographies*, 53.

82. Douglass, *Frederick Douglass: Autobiographies*, 54.

83. Douglass, *Frederick Douglass: Autobiographies*, 65.

84. Douglass, *Frederick Douglass: Autobiographies*, 58.

85. Douglass, *Frederick Douglass: Autobiographies*, 64.

86. Douglass, *Frederick Douglass: Autobiographies*, 65.

87. Henry Highland Garnet, "An Address to the Slaves of the United States," in Levine, Stauffer, and McKivigan, *Heroic Slave*, 109–10.

88. "The Buffalo Convention of Men of Color," *Liberator*, September 22, 1843.

89. McKivigan, *Abolitionism and American Politics*, 171.

90. Douglass, "American Prejudice against Color," in Levine, Stauffer, and McKivigan, *Heroic Slave*, 113–14.

91. Douglass, "American Prejudice against Color," 114, emphasis in the original.

92. Douglass, "Farewell Speech to the British People," 71.

93. Douglass, *The Heroic Slave*, in *Portable Frederick Douglass*, 192.

94. Douglass, *Heroic Slave*, 157.

95. Douglass, "The True Remedy for the Fugitive Slave," *Frederick Douglass' Paper*, June 9, 1854.

96. Garrison, "Declaration of Sentiments of the American Anti-Slavery Society," 79.

97. Douglass, *My Bondage and My Freedom*, 286–87.

98. William Lloyd Garrison, "Letter from Mr. Douglass," *Liberator*, July 23, 1847.

99. Philip S. Foner, *Frederick Douglass*, 78.

100. William Lloyd Garrison to Helen Eliza Garrison, October 20, 1847, in *Letters*, 533.

101. Douglass, *Frederick Douglass: Autobiographies*, 705.

102. Douglass to Gerrit Smith, May 1, 1851, in *Life and Writings*, 2:152.

103. Douglass to Henry Clay, December 3, 1847, in *Frederick Douglass: Selected Speeches and Writings*, 94.

104. New York Liberty Party, *Proceedings of the National Liberty Convention*, 6.

105. Douglass, *My Bondage and My Freedom*, 292.

2. "An Anti-slavery Instrument"

1. Stewart, "A Constitutional Argument on the Subject of Slavery," in tenBroek, *Equal under Law*, 283.

2. Stewart, "Constitutional Argument on the Subject of Slavery," 287.

3. Stewart, "Constitutional Argument on the Subject of Slavery," 288.

4. Stewart, "Constitutional Argument on the Subject of Slavery," 289.

5. Spooner, *Unconstitutionality of Slavery*, 67.

6. Goodell, *Views of American Constitutional Law*, 7.

7. Frothingham, *Gerrit Smith*, 188.

8. Douglass, "Oath to Support the Constitution," 118.

9. Douglass, "Change of Opinion Announced," 174.

10. May, *Some Recollections*, 164–65.

11. May, *Some Recollections*, 400.

12. Frothingham, *Gerrit Smith*, 166.

13. Frothingham, *Gerrit Smith*, 170.

14. Frothingham, *Gerrit Smith*, 175.

15. Gerrit Smith, *Substance of the Speech*, 3.

16. William Lloyd Garrison, "Letter," *Liberator*, October 22, 1858.

17. Frothingham, *Gerrit Smith*, 202.

18. Frothingham, *Gerrit Smith*, 206.

19. George H. Smith, introduction to Spooner, *Lysander Spooner Reader*, ix.

20. Spooner, *Unconstitutionality of Slavery*, 8.

21. Spooner, *Unconstitutionality of Slavery*, 9–10.

22. Spooner, *Unconstitutionality of Slavery*, 70.

23. United States v. Fisher, 6 U.S. 358, 390 (1805).

24. Spooner, *Unconstitutionality of Slavery*, 74, emphasis in the original.

25. Spooner, *Unconstitutionality of Slavery*, 71.

26. Madison, *Notes*, 224.

27. Madison to Robert Walsh, November 27, 1819, in *Writings*, 738.

28. Spooner, *Unconstitutionality of Slavery*, 68, emphasis in the original.

29. Spooner, *Unconstitutionality of Slavery*, 71.

30. Frothingham, *Gerrit Smith*, 190, emphasis in the original.

31. Phillips, *Review of Lysander Spooner's Essay*, 4.

32. Douglass, "The Constitution and Slavery," in *Frederick Douglass: Selected Speeches and Writings*, 128, emphasis in the original.

33. Calhoun, "The Address of the Southern Delegates in Congress, to Their Constituents," in *Works of John C. Calhoun*, 6:292–93.

34. Douglass, "The Address of the Southern Delegates in Congress to Their Constituents, or, the Address of John C. Calhoun and Forty Other Thieves," in *Life and Writings*, 1:354–55, emphasis in the original.

35. Douglass, "Address of John C. Calhoun and Forty Other Thieves," 356–57.

36. Gerrit Smith to Frederick Douglass, February 9, 1849, in Douglass, *Frederick Douglass Papers*, ser. 3, 1:356–57.

37. Douglass, "Constitution and Slavery," in *Frederick Douglass: Selected Speeches and Writings*, 129.

38. Douglass, "Constitution and Slavery," in *Frederick Douglass: Selected Speeches and Writings*, 130–31.

39. Douglass, "Comments on Gerrit Smith's Address," in *Frederick Douglass: Selected Speeches and Writings*, 139.

40. Douglass, "Oath to Support the Constitution," 118.

41. Douglass, "Oath to Support the Constitution," 118–19.

42. Douglass to Gerrit Smith, Esqr., January 21, 1851, in *Selected Speeches and Writings*, 171, emphasis in the original.

43. Douglass to Gerrit Smith, May 1, 1851, in *Life and Writings*, 2:152–53.

44. Douglass, *My Bondage and My Freedom*, 292–93.

45. Douglass, "Is the United States Constitution for or against Slavery?" in *Life and Writings*, 5:196.

46. Douglass, *My Bondage and My Freedom*, 292.

47. Douglass, "Change of Opinion Announced," 174.

48. William Lloyd Garrison, "Letter," *Liberator*, November 18, 1853.

49. Harriet Beecher Stowe to William Lloyd Garrison, December 19, 1853, in Philip S. Foner, *Frederick Douglass*, 151–52.

50. William Lloyd Garrison to Samuel J. May, September 28, 1860, in *Letters*, 693.

51. Douglass, *My Bondage and My Freedom*, 293.

52. Douglass, *Frederick Douglass: Autobiographies*, 800.

53. Hart, *Salmon Portland Chase*, 49–50.

54. Hart, *Salmon Portland Chase*, 50–51.

55. Niven, *Salmon P. Chase*, 68.

56. Chase to Charles D. Cleveland, October 22, 1841, in *Chase Papers*, 2:80.

57. Weld, "The Power of Congress over Slavery in the District of Columbia," in ten-Broek, *Equal under Law*, 276, emphasis in the original.

58. Chase, *Argument for the Defendant*, 75.

59. Salmon P. Chase to Theodore Parker, July 17, 1856, in Parker, *Life and Correspondence*, 2:519, emphasis in the original.

60. Jones v. Van Zandt, 46 U.S. 215, 229 (1847).

61. Chase, *Union and Freedom without Compromise*, 1.

62. Porter, *National Party Platforms*, 24.

63. Porter, *National Party Platforms*, 25.

64. Eric Foner, *Free Soil*, 87.

65. Madison, *Notes*, 390.

66. Madison, *Notes*, 502.

67. Madison, *Notes*, 502.

68. Madison, *Notes*, 503.

69. Madison, *Notes*, 503.

70. Madison, *Notes*, 503.

71. Madison, *Notes*, 503–4.

72. Wendell Philips Garrison and Garrison, *William Lloyd Garrison*, 3:406, emphasis in the original.

73. Philip S. Foner, *Frederick Douglass*, 161.

74. Douglass to Gerrit Smith, Esqr., July 15, 1852, in *Life and Writings*, 2:206, emphasis in the original.

75. Douglass, "The Fugitive Slave Law," in *Life and Writings*, 2:206.

76. Douglass, "Fugitive Slave Law," 207.

77. Douglass, "Fugitive Slave Law," 208.

78. Douglass, "Fugitive Slave Law," 209.

79. Porter, *National Party Platforms*, 33–34.

80. Douglass, "The National Free Soil Convention," *Frederick Douglass' Paper*, August 20, 1852, emphasis in the original.

81. Angle, *Created Equal?*, 111.

82. Angle, *Created Equal?*, 260.

83. Angle, *Created Equal?*, 260–61.

84. Lincoln, "Address at Cooper Institute," in *Complete Works*, 5:320.

85. Lincoln, "Address at Cooper Institute," 321–22.

86. Lincoln, "Address at Cooper Institute," 309.

87. Douglass, "The Constitution of the United States: Is It Pro-Slavery or Anti-Slavery?," in *Selected Speeches and Writings*, 381.

88. Douglass, "Constitution of the United States," 383.

89. Douglass, "Constitution of the United States," 384.

90. Douglass, "Constitution of the United States," 385.

91. Lincoln, "Address at Cooper Institute," 327.

92. Douglass, "Constitution of the United States," 389–90.

93. Douglass, "The Chicago Nominations," in *Life and Writings*, 2:485.

94. Douglass, "Oath to Support the Constitution," 118–19.

3. "Judgment of the Supreme Court"

1. 12 Reg. Deb. 72–73 (1836).

2. Calhoun, *Speech of the Hon. J. C. Calhoun*, 3.

3. Calhoun, *Speech of the Hon. J. C. Calhoun*, 3–4.

4. Calhoun, *Speech of the Hon. J. C. Calhoun*, 12, emphasis in the original.

5. Calhoun, *Speech of the Hon. J. C. Calhoun*, 13.

6. Douglass, "Farewell Speech to the British People," 60.

7. Douglass, *My Bondage and My Freedom*, 266, emphasis in the original.

8. Douglass, "Meaning of July Fourth for the Negro," 191.

9. Douglass, "The Dred Scott Decision," in *Frederick Douglass: Selected Speeches and Writings*, 348.

10. Annals of Cong. 9th Cong., 2nd Sess. 239 (1806).

11. Jefferson to John Holmes, April 22, 1820, *Life and Selected Writings*, 698.

12. John C. Calhoun, "Speech, February 6, 1837," in Briggs, *Noted Speeches of Daniel Webster, Henry Clay, John C. Calhoun*, 132.

13. Calhoun, "Speech, February 6, 1837," 134.

14. Calhoun, "Speech, February 6, 1837," 132.

15. Calhoun, "Speech on the Oregon Bill," in *Works*, 4:501.

16. Calhoun, "Speech on the Oregon Bill," 498.

17. Calhoun, "Speech on the Slavery Question," in *Works*, 4:572.

18. Douglass, "Weekly Review of Congress," in *Life and Writings*, 2:110.

19. Douglass, "Weekly Review of Congress," 111.

20. Calhoun, "Speech on the Oregon Bill," 507.

21. Calhoun, "Speech on the Oregon Bill," 509.

22. Calhoun, "Speech on the Oregon Bill," 511.

23. Calhoun, "Speech on the Oregon Bill," 510.

24. Calhoun, "Speech on the Oregon Bill," 512.

25. Douglass to Horace Greeley, April 15, 1846, in *Frederick Douglass: Selected Speeches and Writings*, 28.

26. Jefferson, *Notes on Virginia*, in *Life and Selected Writings*, 279.

27. Douglass, "Inhumanity of Slavery," in *My Bondage and My Freedom*, 339.

28. Fitzhugh, *Sociology for the South*, iv.

29. Fitzhugh, *Sociology for the South*, 222.

30. Fitzhugh, *Sociology for the South*, 179.

31. "Review," *Southern Literary Messenger*, vol. 21, 1885.

32. Hertz, *Hidden Lincoln*, 97.

33. George Fitzhugh, "Revolutions of '76 and '61 Contrasted," *De Bow's Review*, vol. 4, After the War Series, July–December 1867.

34. Fitzhugh, *Sociology for the South*, 25–26.

35. Fitzhugh, "Revolutions of '76 and '61 Contrasted."

36. Locke, *The Second Treatise of Government*, in *Political Writings*, 274.

37. Douglass, "Friendly Word to Maryland," in *Frederick Douglass Papers*, ser. 1, 4:42, emphasis in the original.

38. Douglass, "To My Old Master," in *Portable Frederick Douglass*, 414.

39. Douglass, "To My Old Master," 415–16.

40. Fought, *Women in the World of Frederick Douglass*, 120, emphasis in the original.

41. Douglass, "Meaning of July Fourth for the Negro," 185.

42. Douglass, "Meaning of July Fourth for the Negro," 188–89.

43. Douglass, "Meaning of July Fourth for the Negro," 189, emphasis in the original.

44. Douglass, "Meaning of July Fourth for the Negro," 194.

45. Douglass, "Meaning of July Fourth for the Negro," 196, emphasis in the original.

46. Philip S. Foner, *Frederick Douglass*, 134.

47. Douglass, "Freedom's Battle at Christiana," in *Frederick Douglass: Selected Speeches and Writings*, 182.

48. Douglass, "Meaning of July Fourth for the Negro," 190.

49. Douglass, "Meaning of July Fourth for the Negro," 192.

50. Douglass, "Meaning of July Fourth for the Negro," 186.

51. Douglass, "Meaning of July Fourth for the Negro," 191.

52. Douglass, "Meaning of July Fourth for the Negro," 191–92.

53. Douglass, "Meaning of July Fourth for the Negro," 201–2.

54. Douglass, "Meaning of July Fourth for the Negro," 203.

55. Tyler, *Memoir of Roger Brooke Taney*, 126.

56. Tyler, *Memoir of Roger Brooke Taney*, 127.

57. Tyler, *Memoir of Roger Brooke Taney*, 130.

58. Charles Smith, *Roger B. Taney*, 141.

59. Swisher, *Roger B. Taney*, 151.

60. Swisher, *Roger B. Taney*, 154.

61. Swisher, *Roger B. Taney*, 158.

62. Scott v. Sandford, 60 U.S. 393, 407 (1857).

63. An Act to Authorize the People of the Missouri Territory to Form a Constitution and State Government (March 6, 1820), *U.S. Statutes at Large* 3 (1846): 548.

64. Fehrenbacher, *Dred Scott Case*, 252.

65. Ehrlich, *They Have No Rights*, 64–65.

66. Ehrlich, *They Have No Rights*, 65.

67. Ehrlich, *They Have No Rights*, 67.

68. Kurland and Casper, *Landmark Briefs*, 3:171.

69. Kurland and Casper, *Landmark Briefs*, 3:188.

70. Kurland and Casper, *Landmark Briefs*, 3:204.

71. Kurland and Casper, *Landmark Briefs*, 3:206.

72. Kurland and Casper, *Landmark Briefs*, 3:207.

73. Kurland and Casper, *Landmark Briefs*, 3:232.

74. Kurland and Casper, *Landmark Briefs*, 3:237.

75. Horwitz, *Midnight Rising*, 54.

76. Sumner, *Crime against Kansas*, 9.

77. Donald, *Charles Sumner*, 243.

78. Richardson, *Compilation of the Messages and Papers of the Presidents*, 5:401.

79. Douglass, "Fremont and Dayton," in *Life and Writings*, 2:398.

80. Douglass, "Fremont and Dayton," 399.

81. Douglass, "Fremont and Dayton," 398–99.

82. *Scott*, 60 U.S. at 403.

83. *Scott*, 60 U.S. at 404.

84. *Scott*, 60 U.S. at 452.

85. *Scott*, 60 U.S. at 572–73.

86. *Scott*, 60 U.S. at 576.

87. *Scott*, 60 U.S. at 407.

88. Thaddeus Stevens, "Thaddeus Stevens on Reconstruction," in Mackey, *Documentary History of Civil War Era*, 2:158.

89. Douglass, "The Kansas-Nebraska Bill," in *Life and Writings*, 2:317.

90. Douglass, "The Claims of Our Common Cause," in *Frederick Douglass: Selected Speeches and Writings*, 264.

91. Douglass, "Dred Scott Decision," 345.

92. Douglass, "Dred Scott Decision," 346–47.

93. Douglass, "Dred Scott Decision," 347.

94. Douglass, "Dred Scott Decision," 348.

95. Douglass, "Dred Scott Decision," 347.

96. Douglass, "Dred Scott Decision," 352–53.

97. Douglass, "Dred Scott Decision," 354.

98. Douglass, "Dred Scott Decision," 349.

4. "To Arms!"

1. Douglass, "The Fall of Sumter," in *Life and Writings*, 3:89.

2. Douglass, "Fall of Sumter," 91.

3. Douglass, "Fall of Sumter," 90.

4. Douglass, "Notes on the War," in *Life and Writings*, 3:114.

5. Douglass to Rev. Samuel J. May, August 30, 1861, in *Life and Writings*, 3:158.

6. Douglass, "How to End the War," in *Life and Writings*, 3:94.

7. Douglass, "Mission of the War," 403.

8. Douglass, "How to End the War," 94.

9. Lincoln to General John C. Frémont, September 2, 1861, in *Complete Works*, 6:351.

10. Lincoln, "Order to General Frémont," in *Complete Works*, 6:353.

11. Douglass, "Fremont and Freedom—Lincoln and Slavery," in *Life and Writings*, 3:174.

12. Douglass, "General Fremont's Proclamation to the Rebels of Missouri," in *Life and Writings*, 3:160–61.

13. Douglass to Hon. Gerrit Smith, December 22, 1861, in *Life and Writings*, 3:184.

14. Douglass, "The Popular Heart," in *Life and Writings*, 3:232–33.

15. Douglass, "I Have Come to Tell You Something about Slavery," 4.

16. Douglass to Hon. Charles Sumner, April 8, 1862, in *Life and Writings*, 3:233.

17. Lincoln, "Proclamation Revoking General Hunter's Order of Military Emancipation," in *Complete Works*, 7:170.

18. Lincoln, "Proclamation Revoking General Hunter's Order of Military Emancipation," 171.

19. Douglass, "The Slaveholders' Rebellion," in *Life and Writings*, 3:256.

20. Douglass, "Slaveholders' Rebellion," 257–58.

21. Lincoln, "Order to General Scott," in *Complete Works*, 6:258.

22. Simon, *Lincoln and Chief Justice Taney*, 188.

23. Ragsdale, *Ex Parte Merryman*, 34.

24. Ragsdale, *Ex Parte Merryman*, 34.

25. Ragsdale, *Ex Parte Merryman*, 35.

26. Catton, *Coming Fury*, 357.

27. Lincoln, "Message to Special Session of Congress," in *Complete Works*, 6:309.

28. Lincoln, "Message to Special Session of Congress," 310.

29. Douglass, "Fighting the Rebels with One Hand," in *Frederick Douglass Papers*, ser. 1, 3:475–76.

30. Lincoln, "Proclamation Revoking General Hunter's Order of Military Emancipation," 172.

31. 12 Reg. Deb. 4047 (1836).

32. Lincoln to Horace Greeley, August 22, 1862, in *Complete Works*, 8:16.

33. Carpenter, *Inner Life of Abraham Lincoln*, 22.

34. Lincoln, telegram to General G. B. McClellan, September 15, 1862, in *Complete Works*, 8:34.

35. Foote, *Civil War*, 692.

36. Holmes, *Touched with Fire*, 64.

37. Chase, *Inside Lincoln's Cabinet*, 150.

38. Lincoln, "Preliminary Emancipation Proclamation," in *Complete Works*, 8:37.

39. Douglass, "Emancipation Proclaimed," in *Life and Writings*, 3:273.

40. Douglass, "Oration in Memory of Abraham Lincoln," in *Frederick Douglass: Selected Speeches and Writings*, 620.

41. Douglass, *Frederick Douglass: Autobiographies*, 792.

42. Douglass, *Frederick Douglass: Autobiographies*, 775.

43. Emilio, *Brave Black Regiment*, 2.

44. Emilio, *Brave Black Regiment*, 3.

45. Douglass, "Men of Color, to Arms!," in *Life and Writings*, 3:317.

46. Douglass, "Men of Color, to Arms!," 317–18.

47. Douglass, "Men of Color, to Arms!," 318.

48. Douglass to Hon. Gerrit Smith, March 6, 1863, in *Life and Writings*, 3:320.

49. Douglass, "Men of Color, to Arms!," 319.

50. Robert Gould Shaw to Francis G. Shaw, March 30, 1863, in *Blue-Eyed Child of Fortune*, 316.

51. Emilio, *Brave Black Regiment*, 33.

52. Garrison, "Declaration of Sentiments of the American Anti-Slavery Society," 79.

53. Emilio, *Brave Black Regiment*, 32.

54. Douglass, "Address for the Promotion of Colored Enlistments," in *Life and Writings*, 3:363.

55. Douglass, "Address for the Promotion of Colored Enlistments," 365.

56. Douglass, "Address for the Promotion of Colored Enlistments," 366.

57. Douglass, "Address for the Promotion of Colored Enlistments," 366.

58. Gooding, *Altar of Freedom*, 38.

59. *War of the Rebellion, Reports*, 13.

60. Emilio, *Brave Black Regiment*, 72.

61. Emilio, *Brave Black Regiment*, 79.

62. *War of the Rebellion, Reports*, 13.

63. *War of the Rebellion, Correspondence*, 203.

64. Cornish, *Sable Arm*, 155.

65. Emilio, *Brave Black Regiment*, 79.

66. Gooding, *Altar of Freedom*, 39.

67. Emilio, *Brave Black Regiment*, 80.

68. Duncan, *Where Death and Glory Meet*, 114.

69. Lewis Douglass to Frederick Douglass, July 20, 1863, in Douglass, *Frederick Douglass Papers*, ser. 3, 2:405.

70. Gooding, *Altar of Freedom*, 40.

71. Gooding, *Altar of Freedom*, 38.

72. Duncan, *Where Death and Glory Meet*, 114.

73. Gooding, *Altar of Freedom*, 38.

74. *War of the Rebellion, Correspondence*, 209–10.

75. Duncan, *Where Death and Glory Meet*, 114.

76. Lincoln to Secretary Stanton, July 21, 1863, in *Complete Works*, 9:37.

77. Lincoln, "Order of Retaliation," in *Complete Works*, 9:48–49.

78. Lincoln to James C. Conkling, August 26, 1863, in *Complete Works*, 9:101.

79. Lincoln to James C. Conkling, August 26, 1863, 102.

80. Lincoln to James C. Conkling, August 26, 1863, 97–98.

81. Lincoln to James C. Conkling, August 26, 1863, 100.

82. Douglass, "How to End the War," 94.

83. Lincoln to James C. Conkling, August 26, 1863, 99.

84. Ulysses S. Grant to Abraham Lincoln, August 23, 1863, Abraham Lincoln Papers, Library of Congress, ser. 1, general correspondence, 1833–1916.

5. "One Nation"

1. Wendell Philips Garrison and Garrison, *William Lloyd Garrison*, 4:160.

2. Douglass, "The Need for Continuing Anti-Slavery Work," in *Frederick Douglass: Selected Speeches and Writings*, 578.

3. Douglass, "Need for Continuing Anti-Slavery Work," 579.

4. Wilson, *Black Codes*, 143.

5. Wilson, *Black Codes*, 96.

6. Douglass, "I Denounce the So-Called Emancipation as a Stupendous Fraud," in *Frederick Douglass: Selected Speeches and Writings*, 713.

7. Douglass, "I Denounce the So-Called Emancipation as a Stupendous Fraud," 712.

8. Douglass, "There Was a Right Side in the Late War," in *Frederick Douglass: Selected Speeches and Writings*, 629.

9. Wilson, *Black Codes*, 63.

10. DuBois, *Black Reconstruction*, 168.

11. Wilson, *Black Codes*, 79.

12. Schurz, "Report on the Condition of the South, December 18, 1866," in *Speeches, Correspondence and Political Papers*, 324.

13. Wilson, *Black Codes*, 75.

14. Schurz, "Report on the Condition of the South, December 18, 1866," 324.

15. DuBois, *Black Reconstruction*, 172.

16. "Mississippi Black Code (1866)," in Bean, *Race and Liberty in America*, 64.

17. *Report of the Joint Committee on Reconstruction*, pt. 2, 57.

18. Civil Rights Act of 1866, 14 Stat. 27 (April 9, 1866).

19. Cong. Globe, 39th Cong., 1st sess., 1118 (1866).

20. Cong. Globe, 39th Cong., 1st sess., 1757 (1866).

21. Cong. Globe, 39th Cong., 1st sess., 1832 (1866).

22. Cong. Globe, 39th Cong., 1st sess., 1833 (1866).

23. Cong. Globe, 39th Cong., 1st sess., 478 (1866).

24. Andrew Johnson, "Veto of Civil Rights Act, March 27, 1866," 314.

25. Andrew Johnson, "Veto of Civil Rights Act, March 27, 1866," 320.

26. Cong. Globe, 39th Cong., 1st sess., 1757 (1866).

27. Cong. Globe, 39th Cong., 1st sess., 2890 (1866).

28. Cong. Globe, 39th Cong., 1st sess., 2542 (1866).

29. Cong. Globe, 42d Cong., 1st sess., app., 84–86 (1871).

30. Cong. Globe, 39th Cong., 1st sess., 2765 (1866).

31. Barron v. Baltimore, 32 U.S. 243, 247 (1833).

32. Cong. Globe, 39th Cong., 1st sess., 2766 (1866).

33. Corfield v. Coryell, 6 F. Cas. 546, 551–52 (C.C.E.D. Pa. 1823).

34. Cong. Globe, 39th Cong., 1st sess., 2765 (1866).

35. Cong. Globe, 39th Cong., 1st sess., 2538 (1866).

36. Douglass, "At Last, at Last, the Black Man Has a Future," in *Frederick Douglass Papers*, ser. 1, 4:271–72.

37. Chase to Stephen Field, April 30, 1866, in *Chase Papers*, 5:89.

38. Lofgren, *Plessy Case*, 67.

39. Kurland and Casper, *Landmark Briefs*, 6:572.

40. Kurland and Casper, *Landmark Briefs*, 6:588.

41. Kurland and Casper, *Landmark Briefs*, 6:590.

42. Kurland and Casper, *Landmark Briefs*, 6:614.

43. Slaughter-House Cases, 83 U.S. 36, 78 (1873).

44. *Slaughter-House Cases*, 83 U.S. at 79.

45. *Slaughter-House Cases*, 83 U.S. at 110.

46. *Slaughter-House Cases*, 83 U.S. at 97.

47. *Slaughter-House Cases*, 83 U.S. at 87.

48. *Slaughter-House Cases*, 83 U.S. at 96.

49. Chase to Cleveland, October 22, 1841, 80.

50. Niven, *Salmon P. Chase*, 447.

51. Douglass to Gerrit Smith, July 3, 1874, in *Life and Writings*, 4:306.

52. Douglass, "What the Black Man Wants," in *Frederick Douglass Papers*, ser. 1, 4:61.

53. Lane, *Day Freedom Died*, 22.

54. Eric Foner, *Reconstruction*, 530.

55. Kurland and Casper, *Landmark Briefs*, 7:288–89.

56. Kurland and Casper, *Landmark Briefs*, 7:319.

57. Kurland and Casper, *Landmark Briefs*, 7:326.

58. Kurland and Casper, *Landmark Briefs*, 7:328.

59. Kurland and Casper, *Landmark Briefs*, 7:329.

60. United States v. Cruikshank, 92 U.S. 542, 552 (1876).

61. *Cruikshank*, 92 U.S. at 553.

62. *Cruikshank*, 92 U.S. at 552.

63. Kurland and Casper, *Landmark Briefs*, 8:355.

64. Kurland and Casper, *Landmark Briefs*, 8:366, emphasis in the original.

65. Civil Rights Cases, 109 U.S. 3, 11 (1883).

66. *Civil Rights Cases*, 109 U.S. at 35–36.

67. *Civil Rights Cases*, 109 U.S. at 36, emphasis in the original.

68. Douglass, "The Civil Rights Case," in *Frederick Douglass: Selected Speeches and Writings*, 691.

69. Douglass, "The Return of the Democratic Party to Power," in *Life and Writings*, 4:423.

70. *Albany Evening Journal*, April 23, 1870.

71. Douglass, "At Last, at Last, the Black Man Has a Future," 266–67.

72. Douglass, "Black Freedom Is the Prerequisite of Victory," in *Frederick Douglass Papers*, ser. 1, 4:54.

73. Douglass, "What the Black Man Wants," 62.

74. Douglass, "What the Black Man Wants," 63.

75. Douglass, "What the Black Man Wants," 62.

76. Stanton, Anthony, and Grace, *History of Woman Suffrage*, 70.

77. Stanton, Anthony, and Grace, *History of Woman Suffrage*, 73.

78. Stanton, Anthony, and Grace, *History of Woman Suffrage*, 73.

79. Anthony, "Appeal for Equal Suffrage," in Stanton and Anthony, *Selected Papers*, 190.

80. Gerrit Smith to Susan B. Anthony, December 30, 1868, in Stanton and Anthony, *Selected Papers*, 200.

81. Stanton, "Manhood Suffrage," in Stanton and Anthony, *Selected Papers*, 194.

82. Stanton, "Manhood Suffrage," 198.

83. Stanton, "Manhood Suffrage," 196.

84. "Meeting of American Equal Rights Association," in Douglass, *Frederick Douglass Papers*, ser. 1, vol. 4, 216.

85. "Meeting of American Equal Rights Association," in Douglass, *Frederick Douglass Papers*, ser. 1, 4:216.

86. "Meeting of American Equal Rights Association," 216.

87. "Meeting of American Equal Rights Association," 217.

88. Anthony, "SBA to Editor, *New York Times*," in Stanton and Anthony, *Selected Papers*, 248.

89. Douglass, "I Am a Radical Woman Suffrage Man," in *Frederick Douglass Papers*, ser. 1, 5:383.

90. Douglass, *Frederick Douglass: Autobiographies*, 802.

91. Gordon-Reed, *Andrew Johnson*, 3.

92. McPherson, *Political History of the United States*, 52.

93. McPherson, *Political History of the United States*, 52.

94. McPherson, *Political History of the United States*, 53.

95. McPherson, *Political History of the United States*, 54.

96. McPherson, *Political History of the United States*, 54.

97. Douglass, "Reply of the Colored Delegation to the President," in *Frederick Douglass: Selected Speeches and Writings*, 588.

98. Douglass, "Reply of the Colored Delegation to the President," 589.

99. Douglass, "Sources of Danger to the Republic," in *Frederick Douglass Papers*, ser. 1, 4:155.

100. Douglass, "Govern with Magnanimity and Courage," in *Frederick Douglass Papers*, ser. 1, 4:144.

101. Trefousse, *Andrew Johnson*, 242.

102. Richardson, *Compilation of Messages and Papers of the Presidents*, 6:564.

103. Douglass, *Frederick Douglass: Autobiographies*, 811.

104. Woodward, *Strange Career of Jim Crow*, 43.

105. Wells, *Crusade for Justice*, 49.

106. Wells, *Crusade for Justice*, 51–52.

107. Wells, *Crusade for Justice*, 65.

108. Wells, *Crusade for Justice*, 61.

109. Wells, *Southern Horrors*, in Wells-Barnett, *Selected Works*, 14–15.

110. Wells, *Crusade for Justice*, 72.

111. Wells, *Crusade for Justice*, 72.

112. Fought, *Women in the World of Frederick Douglass*, 277.

113. Douglass, preface to Wells, *Southern Horrors*, in Wells-Barnett, *Selected Works*, 16.

114. Douglass, introduction to *The Reason Why the Colored American Is Not in the World's Columbian Exposition*, in *Portable Frederick Douglass*, 518–19.

115. Mary Church Terrell, "I Remember Frederick Douglass," *Ebony*, September 12, 1953.

116. Douglass, "Lessons of the Hour," in *Portable Frederick Douglass*, 379.

117. Douglass, "Lessons of the Hour," 377.

118. Douglass, "Lessons of the Hour," 390.

119. Douglass, "Lessons of the Hour," 387.

120. Douglass, "Lessons of the Hour," 380.

121. Douglass, "Lessons of the Hour," 382.

122. Douglass, "Lessons of the Hour," 392.

123. Douglass, "Meaning of July Fourth for the Negro," 203.

124. Douglass, "Dred Scott Decision," 346.

125. Douglass, "Lessons of the Hour," 397–98.

126. Douglass, "Lessons of the Hour," 406.

127. Douglass, "Lessons of the Hour," 407.

Epilogue

1. Douglass, "I am a Radical Woman Suffrage Man," 383.

2. Douglass, "Give Women Fair Play," in *Frederick Douglass Papers*, ser. 1, 5:353.

3. Obituary, *New York Times*, February 20, 1895.

4. Obituary, *Times* (London), February 22, 1895.

5. Wells, *Crusade for Justice*, 72.

6. Douglass, "To My Old Master," 415–16.

Bibliography

Angle, Paul M., ed. *Created Equal? The Complete Lincoln-Douglas Debates of 1858*. Chicago: University of Chicago Press, 1958.

Bean, Jonathan, ed. *Race and Liberty in America: The Essential Reader*. Lexington: University Press of Kentucky, 2009.

Bingham, Caleb, ed. *The Columbian Orator: Containing a Variety of Original and Selected Pieces, Together with Rules; Calculated to Improve Youth and Others in the Ornamental and Useful Art of Eloquence*. Stereotype ed. Boston: J. H. A. Frost, 1832.

Briggs, Lilian Marie, ed. *Noted Speeches of Daniel Webster, Henry Clay, John C. Calhoun*. New York: Moffat, Yard, 1912.

Calhoun, John C. *Speech of the Hon. J. C. Calhoun, of South Carolina, on the Abolition Petitions, Delivered on Wednesday, March 9, 1836*. Washington City: Duff Green, Printers, 1836.

———. *The Works of John C. Calhoun*. Vol. 4. Edited by Richard K. Cralle. New York: D. Appleton, 1854.

———. *The Works of John C. Calhoun*. Vol. 6. Edited by Richard K. Cralle. New York: D. Appleton, 1855.

Carpenter, Francis B. *The Inner Life of Abraham Lincoln: Six Months at the White House*. New York: Hurd and Houghton, 1868.

Catton, Bruce. *The Coming Fury*. Garden City: Doubleday, 1961.

Chapman, John Jay. *William Lloyd Garrison*. New York: Moffat, Yard, 1913.

Chase, Salmon P. *An Argument for the Defendant, Submitted to the Supreme Court of the United States, at the December Term, 1846, in the Case of Wharton Jones v. John Van Zandt*. Cincinnati: R. P. Donogh, 1847.

———. *Inside Lincoln's Cabinet: The Civil War Diaries of Salmon P. Chase*. Edited by David Donald. New York: Longmans, Green, 1954.

———. *The Salmon P. Chase Papers*. Vol 2. *Correspondence, 1823–1857*. Edited by John Niven. Kent OH: Kent State University Press, 1994.

——. *The Salmon P. Chase Papers.* Vol. 5. *Correspondence, 1865–1873.* Edited by John Niven. Kent OH: Kent State University Press, 1998.

——. *Union and Freedom without Compromise: Speech of S. P. Chase, of Ohio, in the Senate of the United States, March 26–7, 1850.* Washington DC: Printed at the Congressional Globe Office, 1850.

Cornish, Dudley Taylor. *The Sable Arm: Negro Troops in the Union Army, 1861–1865.* New York: W. W. Norton, 1966.

Donald, David Herbert. *Charles Sumner and the Coming of the Civil War.* Naperville IL: Sourcebooks, 2009.

Douglass, Frederick. *Frederick Douglass: Autobiographies.* Edited by Henry Louis Gates Jr. New York: Library of America, 1994.

——. *Frederick Douglass: Selected Speeches and Writings.* Edited by Philip S. Foner. Abridged and adapted by Yuval Taylor. Chicago: Lawrence Hill Books, 1999.

——. *The Frederick Douglass Papers.* Ser. 1. *Speeches, Debates, and Interviews.* Vol. 1. *1841–1846.* Edited by John W. Blassingame. New Haven CT: Yale University Press, 1979.

——. *The Frederick Douglass Papers.* Ser. 1. *Speeches, Debates, and Interviews.* Vol. 3. *1855–1863.* Edited by John W. Blassingame. New Haven CT: Yale University Press, 1985.

——. *The Frederick Douglass Papers.* Ser. 1. *Speeches, Debates, and Interviews.* Vol. 4. *1864–1880.* Edited by John W. Blassingame and John R. McKivigan. New Haven CT: Yale University Press, 1991.

——. *The Frederick Douglass Papers.* Ser. 1. *Speeches, Debates, and Interviews.* Vol. 5. *1881–1895.* Edited by John W. Blassingame and John R. McKivigan. New Haven CT: Yale University Press, 1992.

——. *The Frederick Douglass Papers.* Ser. 3. *Correspondence.* Vol. 1. *1842–1852.* New Haven CT: Yale University Press, 2009.

——. *The Frederick Douglass Papers.* Ser. 3. *Correspondence.* Vol. 2. *1853–1865.* New Haven CT: Yale University Press, 2018.

——. *The Life and Writings of Frederick Douglass.* Vol. 1. *Early Years, 1817–1849.* Edited by Philip S. Foner. New York: International Publishers, 1950.

——. *The Life and Writings of Frederick Douglass.* Vol. 2. *Pre–Civil War Decade, 1850–1860.* Edited by Philip S. Foner. New York: International Publishers, 1950.

——. *The Life and Writings of Frederick Douglass.* Vol. 3. *The Civil War, 1861–1865.* Edited by Philip S. Foner. New York: International Publishers, 1952.

——. *The Life and Writings of Frederick Douglass.* Vol. 4. *Reconstruction and After.* Edited by Philip S. Foner. New York: International Publishers, 1955.

——. *The Life and Writings of Frederick Douglass.* Vol. 5. *Supplementary, 1844–1860.* Edited by Philip S. Foner. New York: International Publishers, 1975.

——. *My Bondage and My Freedom.* New York: Penguin Books, 2003.

——. *Narrative of the Life of Frederick Douglass, an American Slave. Written by Himself.* Boston: Anti-Slavery Office, 1849.

——. *The Portable Frederick Douglass.* Edited by John Stauffer and Henry Louis Gates Jr. New York: Penguin Books, 2016.

Duberman, Martin, ed. *The Antislavery Vanguard: New Essays on the Abolitionists*. Princeton NJ: Princeton University Press, 1965.

DuBois, W. E. B. *Black Reconstruction*. New York: Harcourt, Brace, 1935.

Duncan, Russell. *Where Death and Glory Meet: Colonel Robert Gould Shaw and the 54th Massachusetts Infantry*. Athens: University of Georgia Press, 1999.

Ehrlich, Walter. *They Have No Rights: Dred Scott's Struggle for Freedom*. Bedford: Applewood Books, 1979.

Emilio, Luis F. *A Brave Black Regiment: The History of the 54th Massachusetts, 1863–1865*. New York: Da Capo Press, 1995.

Fehrenbacher, Don E. *The Dred Scott Case: Its Significance in American Law and Politics*. New York: Oxford University Press, 1978.

Fitzhugh, George. *Sociology for the South, or, The Failure of Free Society*. London: Forgotten Books, 2012. First published in 1854 by A. Morris.

Foner, Eric. *Free Soil, Free Labor, Free Men: The Ideology of the Republican Party before the Civil War*. New York: Oxford University Press, 1985.

———. *Reconstruction: America's Unfinished Revolution, 1863–1877*. Francis Parkman Prize ed. New York: History Book Club, 2005.

Foner, Philip S. *Frederick Douglass: A Biography*. New York: Citadel Press, 1964.

Foote, Shelby. *The Civil War: A Narrative, Fort Sumter to Perryville*. New York: Random House, 1958.

Fought, Leigh. *Women in the World of Frederick Douglass*. New York: Oxford University Press, 2017.

Frothingham, Octavius Brooks. *Gerrit Smith: A Biography*. New York: G. P. Putnam's Sons, 1878.

Garrison, Wendell Philips, and Francis Jackson Garrison. *William Lloyd Garrison: The Story of His Life Told by His Children*. Vol. 3. *1841–1860*. New York: Century Company, 1889.

———. *William Lloyd Garrison: The Story of His Life Told by His Children*. Vol. 4. *1861–1879*. New York: Century Company, 1889.

Garrison, William Lloyd. *The Letters of William Lloyd Garrison*. Vol. 3. *No Union with Slaveholders, 1841–1849*. Edited by Walter M. Merrill. Cambridge: Belknap Press, 1973.

Goodell, William. *Views of American Constitutional Law, in Its Bearing upon Slavery*. 2nd ed. Utica: Lawson and Chaplin, 1845.

Gooding, James Henry. *On the Altar of Freedom: A Black Soldier's Civil War Letters from the Front*. Edited by Virginia Matzke Adams. Amherst: University of Massachusetts Press, 1991.

Gordon-Reed, Annette. *Andrew Johnson*. New York: Times Books, 2011.

Hamilton, Alexander, James Madison, and John Jay. *The Federalist Papers*. Edited by Clinton Rossiter. New York: Mentor, 1961.

Hart, Albert Bushnell. *Salmon Portland Chase*. New York: Houghton, Mifflin, 1899.

Hertz, Emanuel, ed. *The Hidden Lincoln: From the Letters and Papers of William H. Herndon*. New York: Viking Press, 1938.

Hofstadter, Richard. *The American Political Tradition and the Men Who Made It*. New York: Vintage Books, 1989.

Holmes, Oliver Wendell, Jr. *Touched with Fire: Civil War Letters and Diary of Oliver Wendell Holmes, Jr.* Edited by Mark De Wolfe Howe. New York: Fordham University Press, 2000.

Horwitz, Tony. *Midnight Rising: John Brown and the Raid That Sparked the Civil War.* New York: Henry Holt, 2011.

Jefferson, Thomas. *The Life and Selected Writings of Thomas Jefferson.* Edited by Adrienne Koch and William Peden. New York: Modern Library, 1944.

Johnson, Andrew. *The Papers of Andrew Johnson.* Vol. 10. *February–July 1866.* Edited by Paul H. Bergeron. Knoxville: University of Tennessee Press, 1992.

Johnson, Oliver. *William Lloyd Garrison and His Times: or, Sketches of the Anti-Slavery Movement in America, and of the Man Who Was Its Follower and Leader.* Boston: B. B. Russell, 1879.

Kurland, Philip B., and Gerhard Casper, eds. *Landmark Briefs and Arguments of the Supreme Court of the United States.* Vol. 3. Washington DC: University Publications of America, 1978.

————. *Landmark Briefs and Arguments of the Supreme Court of the United States.* Vol. 6. Arlington VA: University Publications of America, 1975.

————. *Landmark Briefs and Arguments of the Supreme Court of the United States.* Vol. 7. Arlington VA: University Publications of America, 1975.

————. *Landmark Briefs and Arguments of the Supreme Court of the United States.* Vol. 8. Arlington VA: University Publications of America, 1975.

Lane, Charles. *The Day Freedom Died: The Colfax Massacre, the Supreme Court, and the Betrayal of Reconstruction.* New York: Henry Holt, 2008.

Levine, Robert S., John Stauffer, and John R. McKivigan, eds. *The Heroic Slave: A Cultural and Critical Edition.* New Haven CT: Yale University Press, 2015.

Lincoln, Abraham. *Complete Works of Abraham Lincoln.* New and enlarged ed. Vol. 5. Edited by John G. Nicolay and John Hay. New York: Francis D. Tandy, 1905.

————. *Complete Works of Abraham Lincoln.* New and enlarged ed. Vol. 6. Edited by John G. Nicolay and John Hay. New York: Francis D. Tandy, 1905.

————. *Complete Works of Abraham Lincoln.* New and enlarged ed. Vol. 7. Edited by John G. Nicolay and John Hay. New York: Francis D. Tandy, 1905.

————. *Complete Works of Abraham Lincoln.* New and enlarged ed. Vol. 8. Edited by John G. Nicolay and John Hay. New York: Francis D. Tandy, 1905.

————. *Complete Works of Abraham Lincoln.* New and enlarged ed. Vol. 9. Edited by John G. Nicolay and John Hay. New York: Francis D. Tandy, 1905.

Locke, John. *Political Writings of John Locke.* Edited by David Wootton. New York: Mentor, 1993.

Lofgren, Charles A. *The Plessy Case: A Legal-Historical Interpretation.* New York: Oxford University Press, 1987.

Mackey, Thomas C., ed. *A Documentary History of the Civil War Era.* Vol. 2. *Political Arguments.* Knoxville: University of Tennessee Press, 2013.

Madison, James. *Notes of Debates in the Federal Convention of 1787, Reported by James Madison.* New York: W. W. Norton, 1987.

————. *Writings*. New York: Library of America, 1999.

May, Samuel J. *Some Recollections of Our Antislavery Conflict*. Boston: Fields, Osgood, 1869.

McKivigan, John R., ed. *Abolitionism and American Politics and Government*. New York: Garland, 1999.

McPherson, Edward. *The Political History of the United States during the Period of Reconstruction*. Washington DC: Solomon and Chapman, 1875.

New York Liberty Party. *Proceedings of the National Liberty Convention, Held at Buffalo, N.Y., June 14th and 15th, 1848*. Utica NY: S. W. Green, 1848.

Niven, John. *Salmon P. Chase: A Biography*. New York: Oxford University Press, 1995.

Parker, Theodore. *Life and Correspondence of Theodore Parker*. Vol. 2. Edited by John Weiss. New York: D. Appleton, 1864.

Phillips, Wendell. *The Constitution, a Pro-Slavery Compact, or, Extracts from the Madison Papers*. 3rd ed. New York: American Anti-Slavery Society, 1856.

————. *Review of Lysander Spooner's Essay on the Unconstitutionality of Slavery*. Boston: Andrews and Prentiss, 1847.

Porter, Kirk H., ed. *National Party Platforms*. New York: Macmillan, 1924.

Ragsdale, Bruce A., ed. *Ex Parte Merryman and Debates on Civil Liberties during the Civil War*. Washington DC: Federal Judicial Center, 2007.

Report of the Joint Committee on Reconstruction, at the First Session of the Thirty-Ninth Congress. Westport CT: Negro Universities Press, 1969. First published in 1866 by the Government Printing Office.

Richardson, James D., ed. *A Compilation of the Messages and Papers of the Presidents, 1789–1897*. Vol. 5. Washington DC: U.S. Congress, 1899.

————. *A Compilation of the Messages and Papers of the Presidents, 1789–1897*. Vol. 6. Washington DC: U.S. Congress, 1900.

Ruchames, Louis, ed. *The Abolitionists: A Collection of Their Writings*. New York: G. P. Putnam's Sons, 1963.

Schurz, Carl. *Speeches, Correspondence and Political Papers of Carl Schurz*. Vol. 1. Edited by Frederic Bancroft. New York: G.P. Putnam's Sons, 1913.

Shaw, Robert Gould. *Blue-Eyed Child of Fortune: The Civil War Letters of Colonel Robert Gould Shaw*. Edited by Russell Duncan. Athens: University of Georgia Press, 1999.

Simon, James F. *Lincoln and Chief Justice Taney: Slavery, Secession, and the President's War Powers*. New York: Simon and Schuster, 2006.

Smith, Charles. *Roger B. Taney: Jacksonian Jurist*. Chapel Hill: University of North Carolina Press, 1936.

Smith, Gerrit. *Substance of the Speech Made by Gerrit Smith, in the Capitol of the State of New York, March 11th and 12th, 1850*. Albany: Jacob T. Hazen, 1850.

Spooner, Lysander. *The Lysander Spooner Reader*. Edited by George H. Smith. San Francisco: Fox and Wilkes, 1992.

————. *The Unconstitutionality of Slavery*. Boston: Bela Marsh, 1845.

Stanton, Elizabeth Cady, and Susan B. Anthony. *The Selected Papers of Elizabeth Cady Stanton and Susan B. Anthony*. Vol. 2. *Against an Aristocracy of Sex, 1866–1873*. Edited by Ann D. Gordon. New Brunswick: Rutgers University Press, 2000.

Stanton, Elizabeth Cady, Susan B. Anthony, and Matilda Joslyn Grace. *History of Woman Suffrage*. Vol. 1. *1848–1861*. New York: Arno Press, 1969.

Sumner, Charles. *The Crime against Kansas: Speech of Hon. Charles Sumner, in the Senate of the United States, 19th and 20th May, 1856*. Boston: John P. Jewett, 1856.

Swisher, Carl Brent. *Roger B. Taney*. Hamden: Archon Books, 1961.

tenBroek, Jacobus. *Equal under Law*. New enlarged ed. New York: Collier Books, 1965.

Trefousse, Hans L. *Andrew Johnson: A Biography*. New York: W. W. Norton, 1989.

Tyler, Samuel. *Memoir of Roger Brooke Taney: Chief Justice of the Supreme Court of the United States*. Baltimore MD: John Murphy, 1872.

The War of the Rebellion: A Compilation of the Official Records of the Union and Confederate Armies. Ser. 1, vol. 28, part 1. *Reports*. Washington DC: Government Printing Office, 1890.

The War of the Rebellion: A Compilation of the Official Records of the Union and Confederate Armies. Ser. 1, vol. 28, part 2. *Correspondence*. Washington DC: Government Printing Office, 1890.

Wells, Ida B. *Crusade for Justice: The Autobiography of Ida B. Wells*. Edited by Alfreda M. Duster. Chicago: University of Chicago Press, 1970.

Wells-Barnett, Ida B. *Selected Works of Ida B. Wells-Barnett*. Compiled by Trudier Harris. New York: Oxford University Press, 1991.

Wilson, Theodore Brantner. *The Black Codes of the South*. Tuscaloosa: University of Alabama Press, 1965.

Woodward, C. Vann. *The Strange Career of Jim Crow*. 3rd rev. ed. New York: Oxford University Press, 1974.

Index